VOICES:

UNDERSTANDING AND RESPONDING TO THE LANGUAGE OF HEAVEN

VOICES:

UNDERSTANDING AND RESPONDING TO THE LANGUAGE OF HEAVEN

Steve Witt

DESTINY IMAGE® PUBLISHERS, INC.

P.O. Box 310, Shippensburg, PA 17257-0310

"Speaking to the Purposes of God for this Generation and for the Generations to Come."

This book and all other Destiny Image, Revival Press, Mercy Place, Fresh Bread, Destiny Image Fiction, and Treasure House books are available at Christian bookstores and distributors worldwide.

For a U.S. bookstore nearest you, call **1-800-722-6774.**

For more information on foreign distributors, call **717-532-3040.**

Or reach us on the Internet: **www.destinyimage.com**

ISBN 10: 0-7684-2598-0

ISBN 13: 978-0-7684-2598-7

For Worldwide Distribution, Printed in the U.S.A.

1 2 3 4 5 6 7 8 9 10 11 / 09 08 07

DEDICATION

To my wife, Cindy—outside of Heaven, there is no voice that I respect more.

ENDORSEMENTS

In his first book, *Voices: Understanding and Responding to the Language of Heaven*, Steve Witt masterfully coaches his readers to recognize and understand how God speaks to us today. The humor, scriptural insight, and touching real-life examples in this book make *Voices: Understanding and Responding to the Language of Heaven* a gripping and powerful read.

—Steve Thompson
Author, *You May All Prophesy*

Over the years, I have greatly appreciated Steve Witt's ministry, especially in these two areas: practical biblical wisdom in knowing God's voice, and daring to believe and move in the unique vision of destiny that God has for each of us. I am excited that Steve has combined two of his life messages into this very needed book. I especially appreciate that *Voices: Understanding and Responding to the Language of Heaven* takes the reader beyond mere teaching. It is filled with practical examples, exercises, and steps that invite the reader deeper into the grand adventure of walking with God. All those who take seriously

Jesus' words that "My sheep will know My voice" will find *Voices: Understanding and Responding to the Language of Heaven* an extremely helpful tool for every area of their life.

—Marc A. Dupont
Mantle of Praise Ministries

There are few, if any, people on the planet who have such an array of experience, disposition, and intensity of spiritual pursuit as a platform from which to launch such a daring volume as does Steve Witt. Others are writing on the subject and doing well, but none are doing it better! This book will help us all!

—Jack Taylor
Dimensions Ministries
Melbourne, Florida

TABLE OF CONTENTS

FOREWORD

STEVE WITT is the ideal person to write *Voices: Understanding and Responding to the Language of Heaven.* He has set his heart to be a strength and encouragement to the people of God, and because of that, God has entrusted to him understanding of many extraordinary mysteries. Some are unveiled in this book.

As I travel, I frequently hear Steve Witt's name. It is always in the context of integrity, faithful service, and practical Christianity. As one who is what he teaches, Steve is able to instruct and inspire a person into the amazing adventure of knowing God's voice. We have enough theorists; Steve teaches us from the biblical concepts that have been lived out in his life. He has spoken into my life in a profound way, and I am indebted to him for this.

Few subjects carry as much weight as the subject of this book: learning to recognize the voice of God. It is our life. Literally. To establish this fact the Scriptures tell us, *"Man shall not live on bread alone, but on every word that proceeds out of the mouth of God"* (Matt. 4:4 NASB). That which proceeds from God's mouth is what keeps us alive. Not just alive in the sense of survival—it launches us into abundant life!

The Israelites made a fatal mistake when they said, *"Let not God speak with us, lest we die"* (Exod. 20:19). The people of Israel thought they would die if they heard His voice. However, what they did not realize was that the *absence* of His voice was the death they feared.

Voices: Understanding and Responding to the Language of Heaven is a journey, an enjoyable journey, into the world of discovering God through His voice. It is an absolute pleasure to read. The insights will thrill your soul, and the stories will give you joy and courage. This is a must-read.

—Bill Johnson
Bethel Church, Redding, CA
Author, *When Heaven Invades Earth, The Supernatural Power of a Transformed Mind, Dreaming With God,* and *Strengthen Yourself in the Lord*

ACKNOWLEDGMENTS

Special thanks to:

- my family: Megan, Lauren, Ashley, and Joshua for their patience;

- my staff for their extra labors in my times of absence;

- my church for their loving encouragement;

- my brother Chris and my sister Pam for answering all of my phone calls;

- Roger Ames for being a listening ear;

- the HarvestNet team for being a prototype of what it looks like when people hear Heaven together;

- and the many others who have shaped my beliefs in God.

Chapter One

LANGUAGE OF HEAVEN:

Understanding the Language of God

God, who at various times and in various ways spoke in time past to the fathers by the prophets (Hebrews 1:1).

The most important thing in communication is hearing what isn't said.

—*Peter Drucker*

IT was a regular day. I was tired, eager to plop myself down on the sofa. Joshua, my two-year-old son, came buzzing into the room. Even though I was tired, I wanted to cuddle and wrestle with him. After all, that's what fathers do with sons. While lying on the sofa, I began to call him: "Josh, come over here and let Daddy give you a hug."

In the typical fashion of a two-year-old, he replied, "No."

Parents learn early on to adjust the way they say things in order to get a favorable response. This form of negotiation matures in the teen years. This being my fourth child afforded me the opportunity to use well-seasoned manipulation techniques! How do I get my son to come over to the sofa and give me a hug? After some thought I said, "Josh, come *cheg zo blah ma!*" This nonsensical communication continued for several minutes, catching his interest. He approached with great interest, studying my lips, trying to understand what his father was saying. With each garbled communication Joshua came closer, his face twisted with attempts to comprehend. I continued until he got close enough that I could reach and grab him, tickling him frantically. With screams of joy, he began a lifelong pattern of running to his mother, reporting on the antics of his father. Nevertheless, I got my hug!

ALLURE OF MYSTERY

Fathers sometimes use mystery to draw their children closer. Heaven also uses mysteries to draw us closer. All revelation is with the intention of relationship. In the beginning of creation, God said, "*Let there be light*" (Gen. 1:3). God spoke these creative words with the thought that He would walk with man in the cool of the day. Day one of creation was with day seven in sight. The macro to the micro. The big picture of exciting revelation in the form of a puzzle works toward the small relationship to draw the curious, the learner, the disciple. There is a cyclical flow of revelation to relationship to revelation in the understanding of God.

The Bible speaks of the 5,000 followers of Christ, yet it was obvious that their revelation was low. They followed Him mainly to be touched or fed, not understanding the full life that He was offering. Their relationship was therefore limited. They were the type of people who hung around Jesus for what they might get; and God does not rebuke them for this, but rather ministers to them. God loves relationship.

The 70 whom Jesus personally selected and sent out had a bit more understanding. They came back excited that even demons were subject to His name. They liked to move in the power of Heaven. That's invigorating, but more informational than relational. Again, Jesus stays close to the relationship side by reminding them not to rejoice in the "power" but in the fact that their names are written in Heaven. They have a relationship with God—power seems to be a by-product.

The 12 who followed Christ were much closer relationally, therefore affording them more of Heaven's information. Peter declared, "*You are the Christ*" (Matt. 16:16). This is major revelation for a mere fisherman who knew Jesus as a friend. In fact, Jesus stated that flesh and blood had not revealed this to Peter, but the Father who was in Heaven. Peter was hearing Heaven's voice. The closer the relational circle squeezes in toward Christ, the greater the understanding.

INSIDERS

The inner circle of Peter, James, and John were with Jesus on the Mount of Transfiguration. Together they witnessed Jesus' transfiguration, where "*His clothes became shining, exceedingly white, like snow, such as no launderer on earth can whiten them. And Elijah appeared to them with Moses, and they were talking with Jesus*" (Mark 9:3-4).

Wow! Not bad for a prayer outing on the hill! They immediately were distracted by the supernatural encounter and responded in a natural way, wanting to build something in honor of the moment. "*Then Peter answered and said to Jesus, 'Rabbi…let us make three tabernacles: one for You, one for Moses, and one for Elijah'—because he did not know what to say, for they were greatly afraid*" (Mark 9:5-6). Immediately a voice from Heaven instructed them, saying, "*This is My beloved Son. Hear Him!*" (Mark 9:7). Their revelation and understanding was increased due to proximity…being close to Jesus.

John was the closest. He leaned his head on the Lord at suppertime. He was called "the beloved." It is not strange that he experienced and wrote the most puzzling revelation of the Bible: the Book of Revelation. That great information from Heaven was delivered to the closest of Christ's associates.

Typically, revelation creates greater relationship and that relationship will bring greater revelation. When my son is close to me, he can hear my heart beat. He clearly hears my voice. He knows my ways. Pulling up close to God will reveal great mysteries and even provide clear interpretation.

If we are to understand the mystery of our life and interpret our purpose, we must learn the language of our Creator. Many ignore the day-to-day revelations that come through mundane conversations, an unusual experience, a chance relationship, or a surprise opportunity. It takes a curious child to explore, search, and understand. It takes a maturing individual to take that information and forge a future, unveiling a destiny and realizing a dream.

LISTENING BUT NOT UNDERSTANDING

The followers of Jesus were often perplexed. It was clear that there were many times that they did not comprehend what He was saying because it was attached to mystery. They asked Jesus, *"Why do You speak...in parables?"* (Matt. 13:10). Jesus goes on to explain that the ones who will understand Him are the ones who have the "dullness" removed, seeing and hearing His words. If there is understanding, there will be change and healing. The ones who tune in to the secrets of Heaven will be impacted in awesome ways. It is worth the effort. It is worth the challenge.

Glance at a few of these biblical passages regarding responses from followers of Jesus. You begin to wonder if they understood anything that He said!

So they kept this word to themselves, questioning what the rising from the dead meant (Mark 9:10).

But they did not understand this saying, and were afraid to ask Him (Mark 9:32).

Then His disciples asked Him, saying, "What does this parable mean?" (Luke 8:9).

But they did not understand this saying, and it was hidden from them so that they did not perceive it; and they were afraid to ask Him about this saying (Luke 9:45).

But they understood none of these things; this saying was hidden from them, and they did not know the things which were spoken (Luke 18:34).

Then the Jews said among themselves... "What is this thing that He said, 'You will seek Me and not find Me, and where I am you cannot come'?" (John 7:35-36).

Then some of His disciples said among themselves, "What is this that He says to us..." (John 16:17).

So they were all amazed and perplexed, saying to one another, "Whatever could this mean?" (Acts 2:12).

Even the mother of Jesus, Mary, had to ponder and attempt to grip what God was really saying.

But Mary kept all these things and pondered them in her heart (Luke 2:19).

EYES TO SEE

My wife often sends me to the basement...to find food. Early settlers in America had to hunt for food and so do I! Every time I venture to find a can of beans or corn, I start getting nervous. There is good reason for this apprehension. I can't always see what my wife sees.

One day, not long ago, I was commissioned once again to retrieve a can of beans for supper. I passed my 14-year-old son on the way, and he curiously asked, "Whatcha doin', Dad?"

I replied with false confidence, "Getting beans for Mom."

After my reply he made a face that basically conveyed, "Good luck. Better you than me."

He knows; he's been there before. At a young age he is already experiencing the fear that every married man faces: not seeing what is only seen by your wife!

Standing in front of the basement shelves filled with multiple vegetables, soups, and cereals, I began my visible search. Minutes passed, yet I had not spotted the beans. Panic started to settle in, so I recruited my son to help. Together we looked, searched, yet no beans. My wife began calling from upstairs, having expected my return much earlier. Soon I could hear her purposeful descent into the basement to do what she "should have done her-self in the first place." My son, hearing her, quickly left the room.

Man invented language to satisfy his deep need to complain.

—Lily Tomlin (1939–)

I was starting to feel fairly confident, that this time she would see that I had searched hard and sure enough, there were no beans. Bursting through the door, she reached up right in front of me, grabbed the can of beans, and said, "You guys are pathetic."

What had happened? I was seeing, yet I did not see. Is it possible that many signs are around us, many voices speaking, yet we do not see nor hear?

Without realizing it, we are all in a language school. The Creator of the universe is trying to communicate. Why doesn't He just tell us in simple ways that we can already understand? Well, sometimes He does. Most times He acts more like an artistic communicator than a scientist. Ponder this idea: Perhaps the message of the words is only part of His communication. Perhaps His goal goes beyond just the conveying of knowledge and information—He seeks to build relationship. He wants us to look, search, and understand.

When God wanted to talk to His people, He often chose a spokesperson—otherwise known as a prophet. Take Ezekiel for example. God instructs him to cut his hair and divide it into thirds. One-third he should burn, one-third strike with a sword, and one-third throw to the wind. Why didn't God just tell people that judgment was coming and that there are consequences? He's an artist. He searches for interpreters.

Have you ever had a dream that you knew was not a "normal dream"? Perhaps there were symbols and expressions that seemed to be weighted with a message. What did you do? You probably did what others do. You don't understand and you don't take the time to figure it out—which is like casting aside a puzzle piece, not realizing the important part it may play in future connections.

CARS AND BIRDS

In the spring of 2003, I was going through a difficult time. It was the anniversary of my father's death. Each year since his death, I had experienced a recurrence of grief and introspection regarding life and its purpose. This specific year, I had a dream. In the dream, I was in the backseat of a yellow convertible, at night, and God was driving. (Don't ask me how I knew that it was God. It was a dream; you just know these things.) I was enjoying the fresh, warm, summer air when a bird landed on the side of the car. Strange, yet interesting. The bird jumped on my arm, and I began to laugh hysterically. I laughed so hard that I woke up laughing! Realizing that it was only a dream was a disappointing. It felt refreshing.

Going back to sleep, I re-entered the dream. There I was in the car again. This time an announcer spoke loudly over the dream like a verbal banner. The male voice said, "I will never leave you, nor forsake you." When I woke up, I was healed of my grief. I have never had a serious challenge with it again. I believe it was God.

Why all the symbolism? God was using images that were important to me. The yellow car was the 1968 convertible Camaro that my father used to own. What about the bird in the dream? I'm a bird-watcher, and God used the bird as a symbol of joy.

There's another interesting connection to my dream that happened later the next day. I was on my way home from work and was listening to the radio. A "sports talk" host was discussing some insider information he had about one of our sports teams in Cleveland. He said that a little bird had landed on his car and told him! His expression of a joke brought a divine confirmation to what had been spoken to me the night before. The joy I received in the dream was supernatural and brought healing to my broken heart. When I re-entered the dream, God titled it: "I will never leave you nor forsake you." Cool! God even works in the night. He longs to communicate. He longs to heal us. He's a loving father.

Learning a Language

How do we learn what He is saying? What do these voices mean? The truth is, you learn the language of God just like any other language. Here are several things to consider regarding the interpretation of God's language.

Motivation

A passion is needed to learn a language. It's easy to get excited about learning French…especially when you land in Paris! I have been to Mexico many times. One of my more memorable times was when I stayed with a family that spoke very limited English. My 20 Spanish words fell short of helpful communication. All night long we passed an English/Spanish dictionary back and forth with grimaced faces, nervous laughter, and eager hearts. That night's two-hour conversation would have normally lasted only 10-15 minutes. Yet it was time well spent. You become closer to knowing someone if you are eager to speak their language. You listen with a greater sharpness and study to make sure you are communicating clearly. In the same way, you have to be motivated to learn God's language. What treasures might be hidden in His communication to you?

Equipping

In Paris they simply stared when I spoke to them in French; I never did succeed in making those idiots understand their language.

—Mark Twain (1835-1910)

Most training in linguistics begins with a language book. What is a spiritual language book? The Bible serves as our textbook for discovering God's communication style. In it we see that He speaks in parables (stories with hidden meanings), plays on words, songs, images, colors, textures, etc. Each chapter reveals clues in the way that God speaks. Stories of God teaching man to understand His methods are prevalent. He speaks to His prophet Jeremiah and says, "*What do you see?*" The prophet responds with a simple, "*I see a branch of an almond tree.*" Immediately God encourages the learner by saying, "*You have seen well!*" (Jer. 1:11-12). God is a great coach, and He is more willing than you think to help you understand Him! A lifetime of studying the words and ways of Heaven will yield an understanding of Heaven that will bring great peace and joy.

Environment

I lived in Canada for ten years. In order to get a good job in Canada, it is imperative that you learn to speak French because Canada is a bilingual country. Listening to instructional language CDs in your car will only take you so far. I knew many business people whose companies sent them to northern Quebec where only French is spoken. This approach is called "French language immersion." They drop you in a town where very few people speak English, and thus you are forced, due to your environment, to learn French...or starve! Within weeks you have greatly improved in conversational French. It's a radical step to fast-track a learner into the disciplines of language development.

Placing yourself with friends or spiritual comrades who believe that God speaks is a great start to learning the language of Heaven. A landscape of imagination that allows you to share and wonder without ridicule...places of pondering with people of wondering...this is an environment where you can learn. This is where God's language can be deciphered.

Humility

I have learned the hard way that it is humbling to invade different cultures. In England, for example, you might discover, as I did, that saying "pants" instead of "trousers" is a big no-no! Other embarrassing linguistic mistakes that I have blundered through can't be printed in a refined book such as this!

Once, I was in a northern country, which will remain unnamed. My Canadian friend Kim and I were feasting together with a large family from that country after conference meetings.

Earlier that day, Kim and I had been talking about how we would love to have an espresso. We were going through the list of desired hot beverages when we encountered our mutual favorite: mocha! As the great feast was finishing off, Kim and I looked at each other, recalling our earlier conversation. Kim said, "Yep, I'd love to have a mocha!" When he said this, the entire table of people froze in shock. Kim repeated the statement again, unaware of the change of emotional atmosphere. This time several children ran out of the room, holding their ears. The host hastily made her way to Kim and whispered into his ear. Our requests for a "mocha" ceased when we found out it was a vulgar word in their language!

England and America are two countries separated by a common language.

—*George Bernard Shaw (1856-1950)*

Learning other languages and experiencing other cultures can be risky to your pride. Venturing into understanding Heaven's language will require great humility. This is yet another reason why a safe environment is important.

Time

I've been married for 29 years. Early in our marriage, I was frustrated to find that what I meant was not always what my wife heard! How many times have I heard, "But you said..."? I'm not sure whether time wears you down or you actually begin to understand each other's language, but things do change.

Now, a slight glance between my wife and I at a party can communicate, "It's time to go." Nods, winks, and completing each other's unfinished sentences adds to the mystique. Yet, with all the improvement over the years, I still say stupid things sometimes. We are not the same people we were 20 years ago. Our dreams, goals, and even personalities shift like the seashore, and it takes continuous effort to know and understand each other.

"I wish life was not so short," he thought. "Languages take such a time, and so do all the things one wants to know about."

—J.R.R. Tolkien (1892-1973), The Lost Road

If that happens among humans, is it possible that an eternal God might take time to know? He is stable and does not shift, but our perspective and understanding of Him will take an eternity to unwrap. Learn to enjoy the process of discovery. Patience is the key.

Ask, and it will be given to you; seek, and you will find; knock, and it will be opened to you. For everyone who asks receives, and he who seeks finds, and to him who knocks it will be opened (Matthew 7:7-8).

CUSTOMIZED COMMUNICATION

Let's take a look at the ways and means through which God speaks to you. Sometimes, looking back at the People, Places, and Things that inspire you may reveal the fingerprints of God. What are the Top Five "hits" in your heart in each of those categories? For instance, under my own personal category of "People," I can list names that you wouldn't know, yet are easily attached to certain character traits. Most of mine were risk takers, self-starters, and creatively-minded people.

God has fashioned who I am through these people. They are not on my top five list by accident. These people have communicated something into my development. God has probably used them to shape me and mold me, without my knowing that He was involved.

Similarly, God placed specific people in the path of biblical characters to guide them into His purpose. For example, the Joseph of the Old Testament ended up becoming the second-most powerful ruler in Egypt. But his story does not begin with his triumphant ascension to authority. No, that happened after he learned many valuable life lessons, which God taught him through the many people he encountered. Looking over Joseph's life, we can see that he had the opportunity to learn (both positive and negative lessons) from many people: his father, his brothers, the slave traders, various rulers, cellmates, and others. Each one "carried" him to the next place that God had for him. The difficult experiences shaped and humbled him to become a great ruler in Egypt.

Who are the most influential people in your life and what traits have you learned from them? List your top five.

Person   **Trait**

1. _____

2. _____

3. _____

4. _____

5. _____

Places can also be significant. God seems to instill a longing in our hearts for certain places. Those locations can represent aspects of God's communication to us. Bethel was an important location in the Bible because it was connected to an experience, a dream. Jerusalem was the place of the temple and held high regard to Jews.

I have a fond appreciation for Australia and Iceland. Australia speaks to me of openness, adventure, and humor. Iceland brings to my mind such words as: rugged, diverse, and ancient. What are your special places and what do they communicate to you? It could be a country, city, or an unnamed place of existence like the mountains, desert, or coast.

Place	Trait

1. _____

2. _____

3. _____

4. _____

5. _____

Finally, what are the things that speak to your soul? I love coffee shops. I used one as my office for almost eight years. I like the activity, being surrounded by books and the smell of coffee. I also love birds! I'm a bird-watcher. God speaks to me many things through lattes and binoculars! What are the things that stir your soul and what might His communication to you be?

Things	Traits

1. _____

2. _____

3. _____

4. _____

5. _____

Why do these things speak to your soul? What is it that God might be revealing through them about yourself, your destiny, or your relationship with Him? This is an elementary step into understanding God's language to you. Let's take an expanded look into basic communication from God. What are His voices into our life?

Exploring the Voice Questions:

1. What are the leading ways that Heaven communicated with biblical characters?

2. Why is mystery so important to God?

3. What are practical ways that I can practice learning the language of Heaven on a daily basis?

Do It Yourself!

Still yourself in one of your favorite places and see what Heaven may speak to you. Listen for the voice in the realm of Heaven, the things around you, and the still, small voice within.

Chapter Two

POWER OF THE VOICE:

Learning to Understand the Unleashing of Heaven's Voice

...he goes before them; and the sheep follow him, for they know his voice (John 10:4).

I was in a train station clutching my coat to keep warm. It was early spring in Chester, England, and the biting cold was invading my borrowed garment. I had taken the day off to tour this quaint Roman town situated on the Wales/England border. My host had given me a cell phone to call him when I was ready. He had made it easy for me—because I'm an American. I didn't have to punch in his number; I just had to say "home" into the phone and voice recognition would promptly connect me to my host. (It is commonly believed that Americans are dull when it comes to understanding other cultures, and especially with using phones overseas. It turns out that, at least from my experience, that assumption is generally correct!)

I readied myself to call my host. Opening the phone, I spoke the word "home," but it became clear to me that the automated voice didn't understand my non-British accent. My accent makes that word sound more like "holm" rather than "home." There I stood, trying to sound British, over and over again. Others around me were beginning to give me strange looks. Finally, after numerous futile attempts, the automated lady in the phone said, "Thank you," and connected me.

The Bible says that we can "know" God's voice. Our ears need to be trained to know that it is God who is speaking and not another voice. Following other voices could be tragic. The Bible gives specific warnings to those who consult with mediums and the like. (See Deuteronomy 18:9-14.) The Bible constantly challenges us to learn to listen to and heed one voice: His.

OTHER VOICES

There are many voices in our culture today. We hear people from the political left calling for greater compassion for the poor and from the right a platform of family values is touted. Good people are debating issues from homosexuality to abortion and using God as their source. This is a time for discernment like never before.

Today, you have to take health into your own hands. Disagreement on treatments and approaches abound thanks to the explosion of information. Everyone is an expert. Many are extremely passionate about what they believe. People can easily generate and spread fear to others with outcries regarding chlorine in the water, electromagnetic waves that will cause cancer, and steroids in our food supply. It's difficult to know what to do and what voice to listen to.

At the turn of the 21ˢᵗ century, rumors abounded regarding Y2K (A.D. 2000). "Will computers shut down and affect the electrical grid, throwing us into the dark ages?" It sounds silly now, yet millions of Americans were storing beans and water in their basements. Hundreds of millions of dollars were spent in fear of our electrical grid being shut down. Computer consultants made fortunes correcting the glitch that theoretically would shut down computers at the turn of the midnight hour on December 31, 1999. I believe a national sigh of relief occurred at the stroke of 12:01 a.m. on January 1, 2000. We survived, and our microwaves still worked!

In March of 2000, we faced the real challenge. This has become known as the "Dot-Com Crash." During the 1990s many were making what appeared to be easy money on the stock exchange, especially with tech stocks. Novices jumped on board and made decisions to invest entire life savings on new companies that hadn't been proven. This "Dot-Com Bubble" lasted from roughly 1995-2001.[1] With the Internet becoming user-friendly to the average American, big money seemed to be only a click away.

Millions of investors lost billions of dollars in a short time. Many believed a turnaround was inevitable and rode their money all the way to the bottom. This was a major slap to the hand of this cyber generation. Many began to go back to smart business fundamentals, doing the hard labor of investigation, shedding the skin of emotion and spontaneity.

TIME TO DISCERN

There probably hasn't been a time in history like today—where people know so much yet understand so little. It is critical that we learn to discern what is being spoken into our life. I'm thankful for all the coaches and mentors who assist us in interpreting the times, but success in life is going to be determined by your ability to interpret your own destiny. Your health, your money, and indeed your destiny depends on your ability to rightly hear what Heaven speaks.

Like it or not, we all must enter the discipline of judging and assessing our lives. This establishment of wisdom will save lives, fortunes, and eternal destinies. Mike Bickle, an author from Kansas City, wrote about this process in his book, *Growing in the Prophetic,* where he refers to revelation, interpretation, and application.[2] These are the three aspects of discerning and activating what Heaven is speaking over your life.

This is nothing new, however. Educators have used a similar assessment regarding learning for decades. They understand that for educational growth to occur, you must have information, understanding, and application.

Information (or revelation) comes in a variety of ways. In a later chapter, we will explore some of the vehicles that Heaven uses to tutor us in our destiny. Everyone hears from God; we just may not recognize the voice. Discernment is necessary because the Bible warns us about getting our revelation from wrong places.

For these nations which you will dispossess listened to soothsayers and diviners; but as for you, the Lord your God has not appointed such for you (Deuteronomy 18:14).

...The secret which the king has demanded, the wise men, the astrologers, the magicians, and the soothsayers cannot

declare to the king. But there is a God in heaven who reveals secrets... (Daniel 2:27-28).

The source of our revelation is important. If we get our "water" from a "polluted well," unauthorized, then we face the danger of deception. In the United States, the regulations for food and drink are strict in order to maintain the health and safety of the public. It is similar with our source of revelation and information from Heaven. The root will determine the fruit. How do we weigh the voice that we are hearing to know that it is Heaven's and thus will produce the best fruit?

Own only what you can carry with you;
know language, know countries, know people.
Let your memory be your travel bag.

—Alexandr Solzhenitsyn (1918-)

First, we need to agree that Heaven wants to speak to us. Moses dreamed of a day when all God's people would hear and speak God's word (see Num. 11:29). The prophet Joel spoke of a day when old men would *"dream dreams"* and young men would *"see visions"* (Joel 2:28). Both of these are language tools that God uses frequently throughout the Bible. The apostle Peter believed that this prophecy from Joel began coming true in his lifetime (see Acts 2:16-17). We are living in the days that God is speaking through many means, both day and night.

MOM'S VOICE/HEAVEN'S VOICE

I grew up in a house with a mother who heard from Heaven. This had its benefits and its liabilities. Imagine being a teenager with a mom who hears from God! You can't get away with anything! God would always use her to "arrest" me if I was starting to get off track. Her keen sense of discernment spared my life many a time.

Once, when I was away at college, I had come to a point of frustration and decided to give up. I cleaned out my room and packed my car, ready to abandon my vision and direction. My final act of evacuation was to glance into the tiny window of my school mailbox—where I saw a letter.

Curious, I opened the letter, immediately recognizing it as a note from my mom. It was hand-printed in capital letters on a legal page. (This was typical of my mom when she would write something that was from God. Apparently God speaks in capital letters!)

It began with "DEAR STEVE...THUS SAYS THE LORD...." I perused page after page of encouragement and reminders of what had been said over me in the past. Phrases such as: "From your mother's womb..." and "Have I not told you..." were sprinkled about.

I remember chills running down my back as if this was coming directly from above. How did she know what to say? How could the timing be so exact? I folded up the note and proceeded back to my room, eventually completing my education.

God is watching over us. He is a father (or in fact, at times, a motherly figure) who cares and will send the needed encouragement.

He sees even the smallest sparrow fall from the tree, and He knows the number of hairs on our head (see Matt. 10:29-31). He watches and speaks.

What are some of the things that we are listening for? I have broken it down into seven categories. Humbly, I must admit that there may be scores of ways and means and intensities of how He speaks. May these serve as a beginning in your adventure of hearing a fresh voice from Heaven.

PREDICTS THE FUTURE

God is not bound by time. He sees your past, present, and future all in one glance. If we want to peek into our future, then we must be sure that we are hearing the right voice. The Bible forbids exploring other avenues and experimenting with false voices. When He speaks, we will recognize that it is His voice because the message will line up with what He has spoken before—similar character, values, and consistency.

When I was on a flight back from Japan with a friend, we had been bumped up to business class and were enjoying the perks of fresh sushi. My friend is a man known for "hearing from God." He leaned over and said, "You're about to be called back to Cleveland, Ohio." My heart sunk. This would not have been my first choice. Don't get me wrong; Cleveland is an excellent city. It's just that for me it was connected to many memories of pain and rejection that I preferred not to face again.

I had been living in eastern Canada for almost ten years. I had contemplated relocation from Canada before, but to a warmer climate than my birthplace of Cleveland. Besides, it felt like a step backward. If this was from God it would need supernatural confirmation from circumstances or other means that would be undeniable.

I politely acknowledged the prediction and turned to the window to ponder the thought.

The opposite of talking isn't listening. The opposite of talking is waiting.

—Fran Lebowitz (1950-)

I concluded that I would do nothing. If this was the voice of the Lord, then I would receive indication by numerous means to give confirmation. The unsettling thing was that the month previous, when I was in Florida, a "Prophet" who did not know me had said that "geographical relocation" was coming with "new headquartering." Couldn't this happen in sunny Florida or North Carolina just as easily as Cleveland?

Returning to my office several days later, I began the task of working through my phone calls. Curiously, one of the calls was from a man named Tom Hare. I had known of Tom for 15 years and had not really had any serious conversation with him in most of those years. The scary part was that he lived in Cleveland!

I called Tom and quickly found that his motive was to invite me to do a seminar in Cleveland. Seeing the fingerprints of God on this circumstance, I talked my wife into traveling with me.

The seminar was good, and the connections were sweet. While I was there though, an unusual thing happened.

I received a call from a visiting minister on the other side of Cleveland. I knew who this man was but had only had one conversation with him, and that was six years before in Kansas City. My conversation with him was strange to say the least. It was cryptic, mysterious, odd. He spoke in a parabolic tone that left you guessing as to what he really meant. He started off by saying, "I'm in Cleveland and you're in Cleveland!" This wasn't really any great revelation! Then he laughed with an unsettling tone that leaves you with the thought that he knows something that you don't know.

He then went on to talk about my future in the city of Cleveland. I had not shared that possibility with anyone because I had not come to that conclusion myself. He used words that God had used in my life before. (Sometimes the repeating of key words that have been used before can be a hint of God's involvement in the action.) By the end, I realized that this was indeed God and based my plans on it. Four months later I was living with my family in Cleveland, Ohio.

In hindsight, I cringe to think where I might be had I not listened to the multiple hints from God. He used a disparate group of people from several countries in a variety of circumstances to corral me into His purpose.

REVEALS SECRETS

I love history. One of my favorite historical figures is George Washington Carver. Born in 1864, the son of a slave, George was orphaned as a child. When slavery was abolished in 1865, George's "owners," Moses and Susan Carver raised George and his brother Jim as their own children. They taught George to read and write and encouraged him to continue his studies. After attending various schools and colleges, George eventually became a faculty member at Tuskegee University in Alabama and became a sought-after expert in botany and agriculture.

World leaders, such as Mahatma Gandhi and Joseph Stalin, sought George Washington Carver's counsel and expertise. Henry Ford offered him unlimited resources to do research for his company, yet this humble man from the South preferred his little laboratory. It is reported that Thomas Edison once told Carver: "Together, we can remake the world."[3]

Carver was a spiritual man who believed that "science could unlock the secrets of the universe." He helped the Southern economy and aided the poor through his research as well as through his efforts to educate people in such things as soil improvement and crop diversification. It is said that he called his laboratory, "God's little workshop." He began his day with earnest prayers that God would reveal His secrets about the plants and vegetables. Richard Pilant, a man who was instrumental in getting Carver's birthplace recognized as a national monument, wrote that Carver's motive was to "put more food in the bellies of the hungry, more clothing on the backs of the naked, and better shelter over the heads of the homeless."[4]

It is reported that one day Carver went before the Lord and said, "Mr. Creator, show me the secrets of Your universe."

Carver in his laboratory at Tuskegee Institute.

The answer came back, "Little man, you're not big enough to know the secrets of My universe, but I'll show you the secret of the peanut."[5]

This launched him on a life of discovery of the secrets of God. He took that peanut apart, studied its elements, and put it back together, eventually discovering over 300 uses of the peanut. Later he would hold up the sweet potato before God and say, "Show me its secrets." Time and time again, fresh discoveries and new opportunities emerged as God downloaded Heaven's information into this humble man's heart and mind. Carver gave constant credit to God as his source and said that "without God to 'draw aside the curtain,' he was helpless."[6]

But there is a God in heaven who reveals secrets... (Daniel 2:28).

In the late summer of 2002, the Washington, D.C., area was terrorized by a team of snipers shooting innocent bystanders. In a three-week period, the snipers killed ten people and wounded three others. Law enforcement was stymied by the pattern with no immediate hope of capture in sight. This was an incident that needed a revealing of that which was secret.

Close to 50 Christian truckers gathered together to pray for the capture of the snipers. One of those truckers, Ron Lantz, of Ludlow, Kentucky, was due to retire within a week. He was driving on a route that was not his typical one. Listening closely to a national truckers radio show, Ron heard the radio host give the description of the suspects' car. Pulling into a rest stop, Ron spotted the Chevrolet Caprice in which the suspects were sleeping.

Chills went up his back as he compared the license plate with the one stated on the radio. He quickly called 911 and arranged with another truck driver to block the entrance and exit to the rest stop. The suspects were arrested without incident. Truckers responded by saying, "We knew the prayer was going to be answered."[7]

God is the revealer of Heaven's secrets. It serves us well to know Him and learn of His ways. Business deals, potential relationships, and costly purchases—and basically all important decisions—might be well-advised with revelation from Heaven.

Brings Order and Purpose

God framed the worlds by His words. He spoke into a void that was dark and without form (see Heb. 11:3). His first recorded words in history were, *"Let there be light"* (Gen. 1:3). This is the pattern of Heaven. Out of Heaven come words that change formless voids into frameworks.

In recent years, sociologists have been observing a new phenomenon that they call "transitional adulthood." It turns out that young adults are taking longer than their parents and grandparents to settle into careers and lives. We are witnessing more and more people who are going through "quarter-life" crisis. "Who am I? What am I really going to do with my life? What kind of life do I want to live?" A kind of social, formless void has emerged.

Now, more than ever, an understanding of our destiny is imperative. Recent runaway best-seller, *"The Purpose-Driven Life,"* has sold more than 30 million copies, becoming the number one hardback in American history! It sounds to me that there is an epidemic of desire for direction.

Maybe God wants to speak into our "formless voids." What if He said, *"Let there be light,"* through a friend, father, or stranger? How might we change?

Several years ago, a friend of mine named Steve was praying for a young woman. He and his ministry partner were trying to be sensitive to this new friend they had just met. While praying for her, my friend noticed her name tag, which said "Julie." In the shadow of his partner's prayers, stirrings began to happen in his mind.

Now, my friend Steve is a product of the 1960s. The music of that decade has a powerful hold on his (our) generation. While listening to his partner praying for this young woman, he began to hear the 1974 song made famous by Bobby Sherman, "Julie, Do You Love Me."

Steve was trying to be spiritual, yet he kept being interrupted by looping thoughts of "Julie, Julie, Julie, do you love me...." Normally he would quickly expunge these thoughts from his head, yet maybe this time was different. Could this be God communicating?

When his turn came to pray, he shared this impression as if God was speaking.

Steve said, "Julie, I believe God may be saying, 'Julie, Julie, Julie, do you love Me?'"

Immediately, she began weeping. It turned out that the exact same Bobby Sherman song was playing on the radio when Julie's mother was being rushed to the hospital to deliver her years before. Her mother and father consequently chose that name for her.

This song was somewhat of a code, a code of recognition from God to her. It had special emotional meaning. It acted as a "*Let there be light*" moment in her life. She was rescued by this word and sent back on her destiny path.

Many people would call this an "Aha!" moment. These moments are more than just epiphanies of self-realization. These are moments that speak into an area of damaged emotions or destiny, and life instantly appears. That's powerful! In an instant, your life makes sense. This is the power of God speaking from Heaven.

Saint Patrick experienced this power. The man we remember in connection with shamrocks, green beer, and chasing the snakes out of Ireland was actually a person who heard from Heaven. Born and raised in northern England or Wales, he was kidnapped and taken to Ireland. He was sold to a local landowner and for six years lived in the fields as a shepherd with his sheep. Enduring the harshest of conditions, he prayed to God day and night.

One night a voice called him saying, "See, your ship is ready." He began walking, without looking back, for 200 miles. He arrived in Wexford and found a boat headed for England waiting. Patrick boarded the ship, but it was not an easy path for him because immediately upon landing in England, he was recaptured and returned to slavery. Yet, another voice from Heaven came, reassuring him that "Two months will you be with them." Eventually, he arrived home safely back in England, where he began to study to prepare himself for ministry.

Upon completing his studies, he heard a voice once more. This time it was in a dream, and the voice was Irish saying, "We beseech thee, holy youth, to come and walk once more amoungst us."[8] He was being summoned back to the place of his slavery, loneliness, and pain. This voice spoke into his formless void of a heart and revealed his destiny: to convert the Irish to Christianity.

Was this saint led by strange voices of insanity or was his path ordered up by God? God used Saint Patrick to drive paganism from Ireland and to convert it to Christianity. Patrick was able to speak over the formless void of Ireland and say, "Let there be light!" Patrick heard a voice, but eventually he *became* a voice.

BRINGS LIFE

The Bible tells us that there is "*death and life*" in the "*power of the tongue*" (Prov. 18:21). We have all experienced both sides of this power. For example, words from someone you respect have the power to lift you to unimaginable heights of esteem or plunge you into the darkest depths of discouragement.

An ancient prophet, Ezekiel, found himself in the midst of a great valley full of bones. These were not just regular bones. These bones were very dry, completely without life. God asked the prophet a question, "*Can these bones live?*" The prophet wisely answered, "*O Lord God, You know*" (Ezek. 37:3).

I can find myself full of doubt sometimes. In those times, I ask myself similar questions. I look at our culture, marriages, and broken family relationships and ask, "*Can these 'bones' live?*"

When Heaven speaks, it has the full potential to bring life. He will use those around us and even ourselves to encourage us.

God instructed the prophet to speak over the bones saying, *"O dry bones, hear the word of the Lord!"* (Ezek. 37:4). When Ezekiel obeyed and spoke those words, something powerful was released. A great noise of bone coming to bone was heard with flesh appearing, yet still there was no life.

Upon further instruction, Ezekiel spoke to the wind to breathe on them and instantly life began to fill this great army that appeared. God interprets this prophetic activation, as He says to Ezekiel: *"Son of man, these bones are the whole house of Israel. They indeed say, 'Our bones are dry, our hope is lost, and we ourselves are cut off'"* (Ezek. 37:11).

This ancient story speaks of the power of our words. Those who have lost hope can now have life again. The words that Ezekiel spoke raised them up into an army, which indicates that a new destiny can also be placed within you.

Once, I was speaking at a conference in Toronto, Canada. On this particular day I was doing a workshop with about 900 in attendance. The atmosphere was thick with anticipation. Speaking on the "Power of Blessing," I began to think of a way to truly encourage everyone. I decided to form an "encouragement or blessing tunnel." One hundred leaders came up front and formed a tunnel by facing one another, 50 people on each side. At first, people were understandably hesitant to go through the tunnel. After careful explanation that these "tunnel people" would speak good, encouraging words over them as they passed through, this emotional "car wash" began.

Several hours later, the line was still proceeding through the meandering conduit. People had become overwhelmed with emotional relief and spiritual healing. Some had to be escorted through, being exhausted with emotion. Many were not used to the power of encouragement and the impact it even had on their physical bodies. Toward the end of the time, I noticed one older lady having unusual amounts of fun. It appeared that her "*dry bones*" were coming to life. Her face was as radiant as an angel.

As she approached me, she almost appeared intoxicated. After speaking with her, I realized that she was simply overjoyed at the experience. Her story poured out of her: years of rejection from mother, siblings, then her own children. She said, "I have been cursed my entire life, but today I received a hundred blessings." She then told me it was her 75th birthday. Being caught up in the excitement myself, I yelled, "Go through the tunnel again!"

What a sight it was to watch this lady receive another hundred blessings. About ten feet into the tunnel, she collapsed, quickly being resurrected by several beefy men who then helped her to complete the journey. Her face was shining as she absorbed every word like a sponge.

Words that bring life are somewhat rare these days. Sometimes, you have to speak words of life into yourself. This will sound strange, but sometimes I call my own voicemail and leave messages. I'll say things like, "You have a destiny. You will be a success. God is with you!" Inevitably, I forget about the "self-encouragement" until later when I retrieve my voicemail. For example, Monday rolls around after I've had a tough weekend. The Monday "blahs" hit me with a vengeance and, discouraged, I call to listen to my messages. I hear the automated voice say, "You have seventeen messages." Fortunately, somewhere in these messages is a hidden word of life. Suddenly, my own voice comes on the machine, speaking forgotten encouragement, bringing life to my soul! Even our own words and thoughts will guide our destiny.

BRINGS VICTORY

Words can become weapons. The Bible says that *"death and life are in the power of the tongue"* (Prov. 18:21). We can build up with words, and we can tear down with words. Jesus Himself came to proclaim a *year* of favor and a *day* of judgment. The ratio is 365 to 1. Judgment words should be prefaced with multiple words of encouragement. The truth is that most of us survive life with few encouragements and immense judgment.

The Bible says that we can wage a good warfare by the words that have been spoken over us. Has anyone ever said something to you that was supernaturally encouraging? It is likely that this was a word from Heaven. Dreams, encouragements, and experiences that give energy and courage are more likely to have good as their origin than evil.

You've probably heard psychologists refer to "self-talk." This is the inward communication that is transpiring in your mind 24 hours a day and determines much of your decision-making process. It is what you really believe about yourself. This is the little voice that tells you whether you are more or less, smart or stupid, able or unable.

This inner voice has been fashioned mainly in your environment. Parents can make comments that burn into your emotional hard drive and become echoes throughout your life. Coaches, teachers, and friends add to the database of endless opinions that help form who you really are. It is like a "video store" of your mind; it contains drama, comedy, action, and romance. The emotional DVDs that you "check out" in a given circumstance will determine your success.

Words that you hear from God are meant to over-ride the backlog of negative experiences. It becomes essential to write down and keep record of good things and words that have been spoken over your life. I have actually created a tape of numerous words that I believe are from Heaven that have been spoken over me. It has become a secret weapon that I deploy periodically. It is amazing the results that I get! When I encounter a difficult challenge, I am bombarded with negative self-talk. It can cripple me. It has hellish energy to emasculate my courage. At these times, I pull out my secret encouragement that eradicates the enemy of my soul.

This charge I commit to you, son Timothy, according to the prophecies previously made concerning you, that by them you may wage the good warfare (1 Timothy 1:18).

BRINGS PURIFICATION

Words from Heaven can arrest you in your tracks. Heaven's words can be a fire on the tender wood of our soul. In 1988, I was living in Canada and was going through a difficult time—dealing with bad weather, broken friendships, futility, and remorse. A friend called from sunny Arizona offering me a job. Immediately, I thought, *Hmm, Arizona has over 300 sunny days a year.* Looking out the window, I began to believe that God was rescuing me. He wasn't.

Quickly, this fantasy of abandoning my vision for a better offer took root in my mind. I became relieved immediately. There is such a thing as "false peace." I was experiencing it.

Through a series of experiences I encountered a man who was visiting from the States. When I introduced myself to him, he made an unusual statement that was not your typical greeting. He said, "Hi, my name is Kevin, and if you do what you are thinking about doing, it will be hell on earth." Immediately, Arizona came to my mind. God was arresting me. My temporary peace left, and I emotionally unpacked my bags.

Six months later, the deal that had been offered in Arizona fell apart. If I had left Canada, I would have missed some of the greatest opportunities of my life, which had not yet been revealed. It would have been easy to ignore the warning. After all, it came through someone I did not know and went against emotions and logic. Yet God can see into the future and attempts to warn us of unnecessary pain.

God used a 26-year-old woman to arrest a notorious killer in Atlanta, Georgia. Brian Nichols was on the run in March of 2005. He had killed a judge and several others. Evading the Georgia police and the FBI, he sought refuge in a randomly selected apartment complex. There Nichols accosted Ashley Smith, a young single mother, and forced his way into her apartment with threats to her life. Bound by tape and cords, Ashley Smith began a relatively calm discourse with her captor.

In the ensuing hours, this courageous woman began to talk with the murderer about God, using the Bible and a recent best-selling book, *The Purpose-Driven Life.* Sharing her personal story about her own husband's stabbing death four years earlier apparently began to warm the heart of this killer.

Ashley began to talk to him about his purpose in life. He said that she was an angel sent from God, and that she was his sister in Christ. He went on to say that he was lost and that God had led him right to her to tell him that he had hurt a lot of people.

Several hours later this man who had caused the largest manhunt in Georgia's history was surrendering without incident. Ashley's words pierced his heart, leading him to stop the violence and surrender to God's will. Her words were from Heaven, melting, purifying, and arresting a wandering soul.[9]

Brings Encouragement

The most common purpose for a word from Heaven is encouragement. God is an encouraging God. Listen to the way He talked to Jacob. Keep in mind that God spoke these words after Jacob tricked his brother out of the family fortune and deceived his father by imitating his brother.

Behold, I am with you and will keep you wherever you go, and will bring you back to this land; for I will not leave you until I have done what I have spoken to you (Genesis 28:15).

God is full of encouragement. Through the Bible He encourages and forgives murderers, thieves, prostitutes, and adulterers. God-given words will bring you to your feet (see Ezek. 2:2). An ancient proverb says, "*A word spoken in due season, how good it is!*" (Prov. 15:23b).

I was teaching communications and human relations in the 1980s for an international training course. I had 44 business people who were under my instruction for 14 weeks. Session seven was peculiar training for business. It seemed more fitting in a church or pop psychology evening class at the high school. It was training on "how to encourage at the workplace."

As an instructor it was my responsibility to demonstrate the principles we were attempting to teach. I had to publicly activate encouragement with several class members. Looking across the room, my eyes landed on Jerry (not his real name). Jerry was the youngest student in the class, barely in his 20s. He had obvious issues of insecurity. His body language was sunken, closed, hidden from the light. He was a dangerous choice. What if nothing happened? What if he was "unencouragable"?

Pointing to him, I began my 15-second encouragement. I told him that I saw courage in him and then gave an example from the week previous to re-enforce my assertion. I was scraping bottom. I was speaking into his potential, ignoring the visible. As I spoke, I sensed a strange empowerment come over me and extended the encouragement to last a full minute. (Sometimes you've got to break the rules!) He was visibly shaken with tears filling his eyes. The encouragement was like water on dry ground.

The class broke out into applause and cheering. A lasting silence followed the applause as if everyone had just had a good meal and were sitting back to bask in the moment. A hand sheepishly arose from a successful banker in the back. This was a man who gave no hint of needing encouragement. His rough, business demeanor had seemingly served him well in achieving his career goals, yet a soft humble voice emerged from him, saying, "Could you do that to me too?" Hands and voices erupted around the room as grown men and women sought for encouragement.

What would happen if we began to release encouragement to those around us? The fear that plagues the business world and personal worlds of many would be turned right-side up! Words would have the power to rescue many from the edge of disaster. If only...

Exploring the Voice Questions:

1. How have some of the expressions of Heaven's voice manifested themselves in your life?

2. What other historical figures exhibited an ability to hear beyond the generation that they inhabited? Might God have been speaking through them?

3. Why has there been such a stigma attached to "hearing a voice from Heaven"?

Do It Yourself!

Speak Scripture over one another in a group to get yourself used to how and what God communicates. Familiarize your language with that of the Bible.

Endnotes

1. Information retrieved on the Internet at: http://en.wikipedia.org/wiki/Dot-com_bubble.

2. Mike Bickle, *Growing in the Prophetic* (Lake Mary, FL: Charisma House, 1996), p. 169.

3. Information retrieved on the Internet at: http://vision.org/visionmedia/article.aspx?id=703.

4. Information retrieved on the Internet at: http://vision.org/visionmedia/article.aspx?id=703.

5. Pat Robertson, *Secret Kingdom* (Nashville, TN: W Publishing Group, 1994), p. 126.

6. Information retrieved on the Internet at: http://vision.org/visionmedia/article.aspx?id=703.

7. Information retrieved on the Internet at: http://www.truthorfiction.com/rumors/s/sniper-driver.htm.

8. Thomas Cahill, *How the Irish Saved Civilization* (New York: Doubleday/Nan A. Talese, 2003/1995).

9. Ashley Smith, *Unlikely Angel* (Grand Rapids, MI: Zondervan, 2005).

Chapter Three

VOCAL VEHICLES:

Learning the Ways and Means of Heaven's Voice

But God has revealed them to us through His Spirit. For the Spirit searches all things, yes, the deep things of God (1 Corinthians 2:10).

HEAVEN has many vehicles that it uses to deliver the messages of hope, warning, and encouragement. Recently, I was about to travel to Scotland. I was going to speak to a group that had great hunger to hear God. The night before I left, I had a dream.

In the dream, I was in a Scottish castle. I had just walked out onto a high balcony, enjoying the rare Scottish sunshine. As I turned to walk back in, I saw a bulldog approaching me with questionable intent. I reached into my pocket and threw something to temporarily distract him. As the dog chased the item, I stepped back out onto the balcony and spied a grassy ledge to hide on. I crept out onto this narrow ledge, leaning on the roof of the building, hoping to escape the dog's notice.

Standing in this precarious position, I looked down to see that I was three or four stories above the ground. I remember thinking, *If I fall down from here, my wife will wonder, "What was he thinking?"* I then woke up.

Normally, I might forget or disregard a dream like this, but something inside alerted me. I interpreted the dream to be a warning to not *shy away* from intimidation, because it could threaten my life. I needed to face the bulldog and not hide. This dream message acted as an empowerment when I went to Scotland. I was keenly aware of spiritual attempts to bully me, and I responded with courage.

(An interesting note: When I arrived in Scotland, I was told about a young man who had just fallen from a castle and was in critical condition.)

Dreams are often ignored, yet they can be a vehicle for enormous revelation. The vehicles that God uses to deliver His messages bring one of three things: revelation, impartation, or inspiration. Ultimately, His vehicles deliver change or transformation that leads to activation. Consider the diagram:

All of God's vehicles deliver a change agent. The battle of the ages is over our restoration to, and understanding of, God. God's strategy is that we may know Him and His ways. Forces in hell and on earth battle to keep us from knowing Him. Whatever God speaks to you is for the purpose of your conformity to His plan for you. Daily messages and change agents are being sent to conform and transform you into the person He wants you to be.

There are eight general categories of His vehicles that I have found, yet infinite expressions of His message to you from Heaven.

CYCLE OF REVELATION

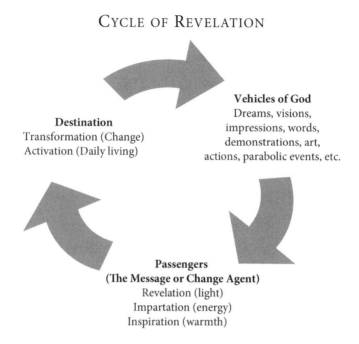

Destination
Transformation (Change)
Activation (Daily living)

Vehicles of God
Dreams, visions,
impressions, words,
demonstrations, art,
actions, parabolic events, etc.

Passengers
(The Message or Change Agent)
Revelation (light)
Impartation (energy)
Inspiration (warmth)

VEHICLES OF GOD: DREAMS

The first vehicle, possibly the most prominent in the Bible, is dreams. Earlier in my life I used to discount dreams; after all, I'd heard many people describe incredibly wacky dreams that didn't seem to make any sense at all. However, the understanding that I've gained in recent years has helped me reap an enormous benefit in paying attention to my dreams.

There are three basic types of dreams. Some dreams are from God, containing warnings, instructions, or encouragements to carry on. Other dreams come from a dark side and are meant to discourage, demean, or "slime" you. Many violent or sexual dreams will fall into this category. Still other dreams fall into what I call "garbage" dreams. These are dreams of the mind that are produced every night to help you "take out the informational/emotional trash" of the day. It is the mind's way of deleting information that is not useful. These dreams are silly, nonsensical plays running through our heads that leave us without the same sense of purpose that others have. Some have called these "pizza dreams," suggesting that what we eat before we go to bed may impact our thoughts. These dreams are weird arrangements of people, places, and events that leave us with no tangible interpretation.

Dreams appear to be connected to REM (Rapid Eye Movement) sleep. Approximately one-and-a-half to two hours every night we have REM sleep. Tests have shown that people awakened from REM have a greater tendency to remember their dreams. We all dream, but we may not always remember our dreams. Freud felt that dreams were a braid of repressed wishes; but Nobel-prize winning scientist Francis Crick suggested that dreams were a way of "sloughing-off each day's meaningless events."[1]

Dreams—Key for Understanding

In the Bible, Daniel describes dreams as *"visions of his head, while on his bed"* (see Dan. 2:28). Dreams play a key part in the biblical dramas. In the Old Testament, Joseph dreams about his ultimate destiny. Daniel receives a dream for a great king that leads to having his life spared and brings him great promotion. The earthly father of Jesus, Joseph, received a dream encouraging him to take Mary as his wife. The wise men who came to visit Jesus at His birth were warned in a dream regarding travel plans. The Bible is replete with examples of mystical, symbolic, literal, and practical communication from Heaven regarding destinies and directions.

Understanding dreams is a lifelong challenge. Biblical dreams fall into three basic categories: literal, symbolic, and revelatory. Revelatory dreams turn the lights on! You get revelation. God gave a man named Abimelech a dream warning him that a woman he was about to engage intimately was already married! That's needed revelation!

Evaluating Dreams

Several things need to be considered in evaluating dreams. If it's a literal dream, then all of the dream must make sense and fit with the circumstance and setting. Most dreams are not literal; therefore you need to consider the symbolism. What is the setting of the dream? Does this setting have special meaning to me? Is it a place in my past? We must also look at the people involved. Are they symbolic of authority, music, family, etc.? I have found that the mood of the dream is important also. What were you feeling: fear, excitement, sorrow, peace?

Finally, one of the best ways to begin interpreting a dream is to ask yourself what the "simple message" of the dream was. Try not to get too complicated. What is your "gut impression" of the message of the revelation? Daniel sought God as to the understanding of a dream. It would serve us well to ask God for help in interpreting anything we get while we are sleeping—especially when the message seems to be about directional changes!

A "Pep Rally" Dream

Several years ago, I was getting ready to begin a church from scratch in Cleveland, Ohio. I had been "planting" churches for a number of years and was going back and forth about what method or values I would use in this particular church. During the summer of 1996, I had a dream that I was speaking in a large, circular auditorium. I was leading people in a pep rally cheer. I said, "Give me an R!" The crowd roared: "R!" And I continued going back and forth with the crowd yelling out the following letters: R-E-S-P-E-C-T. I concluded with: "What does that spell?" The crowd yelled: "Respect!" I woke up with an assurance that this was the underpinning of everything that we would do in Cleveland. Dreams can have great power in giving direction, yet we must not forget that they need careful interpretation.

Historic Dreams

One of the great interpreters of a dream in American history was Martin Luther King Jr. He is one of my favorite historical figures. He served as a "tipping point" for the advancement of civil rights in America. On August 28, 1963, Dr. King stepped to the podium under a cloudless sky. His aides had encouraged him to not share his dream. They felt he had overused the term in other writings and speeches, so instead he crafted a speech called, "Normalcy Never Again."

Dr. King was a dreamer though. Some observers said that he had finished his speech and was ready to sit down when he turned his speech over and leaned back, looking at the 250,000 people present. Allegedly, gospel singer Mahalia Jackson cried out, "Tell them about your dream, Martin! Tell them about the dream."[2]

Arguably, one of the greatest speeches in American history ensued. It was probably not a literal dream, but a prophetic picture of what could be—what might exist. The power of that dream has changed a nation and will continue to have reverberant effects throughout history.

So many of our dreams at first seem impossible, then they seem improbable, and then, when we summon the will, they soon become inevitable.

—Christopher Reeve (1952-2004)

Dreams have power, whether of the literal type or the figurative. The communication and interpretation of those dreams can impact an entire government and the destiny of nations! Dr. King had heard a voice from Heaven, and he delivered the message with passion and conviction, cutting to the heart of racism in America. The power of dreams is so strong that many will try to silence it—Martin Luther King Jr. was shot by an assassin. Yet the subsequent continuation of King's message proves that you can silence the man, but the dream continues to speak.

VEHICLES OF GOD: VISIONS

The Bible is full of examples of visions. At the time of Jesus' birth, the shepherds were led by a vision. In the Book of Acts, a man named Cornelius feared God. Although not a religious person, still he caught God's attention. Cornelius had been faithfully giving to the poor and praying. All of a sudden an angel appeared to him in a vision and called his name. The angel gave him specific instructions as to what to do and where to go.

This becomes a defining moment in the Bible. This is the critical point where the message of Heaven extends beyond the borders of Jewish understanding and gushes into the culture of the Gentiles. This vision becomes the turning point of the New Testament. One faithful man who hears from God is responsible for millions coming to know the voice of Heaven. How did God inform him? Through a vision.

Visions are supernatural. Some people have used the terms "open-eyed" visions and "closed-eye" visions to clarify encounters. This simply refers to whether you witness something with your "mind's eye," your blessed imagination, or you have a literal flesh-and-blood encounter with a supernatural message.

It appears that Cornelius actually saw—with his human eye—a living entity, and it brought him great fear. I can't say that I blame him. Angels are awesome beings in the Bible that have been known to destroy entire cities.

Later on in the same passage, the apostle Peter goes into a trance while waiting for dinner! He sees a vision of a sheet coming out of Heaven. The sheet was full of animals that Peter was not permitted by law to eat, yet a voice said, "*Rise, Peter; kill and eat*" (Acts 10:13). This is a great puzzle to his Jewish mind and is repeated several times. In this instance, God used symbolism and code to communicate what He had already begun in Cornelius. Peter would have been resistant to the expansion of the gospel to non-Jews, yet due to this vision he gets an epiphany that God has cleared the way to include *everyone*.

The vision served as a confidence builder for Peter as he faced some serious challenges not long afterward. Sometimes God has to deliver His word with intensity so that we won't be tempted to forget it. He speaks with the still, small voice all the way up the intensity scale to literally transporting people in the Bible to serve His purpose. That's intense!

VEHICLES OF GOD: IMPRESSIONS

This is possibly the most common means of sensing Heaven's voice today. It is a strong sense that sometimes goes unnoticed. It can manifest in those who do not even know God. I believe it is the root of what we would refer to as "women's intuition" or "gut instinct." Instinct, intuition, and "gut" impressions are raw yet powerful forces that might be nudges from Heaven.

Sometimes this stirring, which takes place deep in our heart, leads people to do wild things. It's that "what if" impression that prompted people in the Bible to climb trees, push through crowds, tear roofs off, and face public ridicule just to get into the atmosphere of Jesus.

Every person who is spiritually maturing begins to recognize the gentle tug in their heart. It can come as a picture, a word, a solution, or infinite other forms. Moving on the "feeling" takes training and courage. You may walk into an office and sense that someone isn't doing well. They may look fine, but something inside says that circumstances aren't good. We usually pass this off as our own mind or emotions, but it could be coming from God.

Jesus moved with impressions and spiritual knowledge. The Bible says that He "*knew their thoughts*" and "*perceived in His spirit*" (Matt. 12:25; Mark 2:8). It seems clear that He was moving in the paranormal or outside natural or scientific laws. He had impressions and responded to them with action or words.

This can be a dangerous area if a person is not grounded in an absolute. Proper programming of your spirit is necessary to prepare you for these spontaneous and sporadic impressions. The music you listen to and the books you read all serve as input for the hard-drive of your spirit. The Bible is a great collection of what God has already said, and it is necessary in the training of your spirit so that clarity and alignment happens when you communicate.

VEHICLES OF GOD: REVELATORY WORDS

This vehicle, revelatory words, is closely associated with impressions. Words are like keys, and we use many of them. Words are plentiful, but words that originate in Heaven have power to change a situation. I was speaking in Japan some years ago. Sometimes before I begin my talks, I like to look over the crowd and see if I get any impressions for people. I always tell people that whatever I share is delivered with an "open hand." This means that it is not a "sure" word but must be judged by the individual receiving it. A "closed fist" word is one that is presented in such a way where there is no option for the recipient. I'm not against this, but I do offer this warning: The deliverer of the word had better *know* that they are hearing from Heaven. I tend to err on the side of caution allowing maximum freedom to receive or reject. My job is to simply speak up!

Anyway as I looked over the crowd in Japan, my eyes were drawn to a young 20-something girl. A phrase entered my heart: "for export only." That's all that came to me, so I shared it.

Delivering words is sometimes like "clicking" on a computer icon. When you "click" on a word, another window opens up. This is the faith element in sharing. You may only get the head-line. The story will come when you read the headline!

Using the Japanese interpreter, I asked the young girl to stand. When she stood, I stated the simple phrase. She looked around puzzled and began to weep. Instantly, another word came to me: "India," so I spoke it also. Great sobbing continued as friends gathered around to support her.

Only later did I find out that she had a life dream of moving to India and helping the poor. She had been diligently working at a local restaurant saving money, but was always falling short. The day before she had spoken to a friend and had basically given up on the dream. The last that I heard, she was on her way to India. Words from Heaven can, at the very least, encourage—and at the most, *transform!*

VEHICLES OF GOD: DEMONSTRATIONS

A quick look at the Bible shows us the creativity and diversity of Heaven's communication. God is definitely an artist...just look around! He loves detail, color, and texture, and other visual demonstrations. The Bible tells the story of a man named Agabus, who has a word of warning for the apostle Paul. Rather than telling the revelation with words, he chose to demonstrate it. He took off Paul's belt and bound his own hands and feet, then proclaimed, "*Thus says the Holy Spirit...*" (Acts 21:11).

Most studies show that learning doubles when we can see the message rather than just hearing it. God must know this. He selects visual aides as a key vehicle throughout the Bible. When delivering His word to Abraham, He took him outside to see the stars and said, "*So shall your descendants be!*" The last book of the Bible is Revelation, where He speaks with great symbolism to communicate His message in pictures and images. Jesus Himself loved word pictures, or parables, which He used in teaching.

FEET TO FEET

I've experienced this form of communication—the vehicle of "demonstration"—many times in my life. Several years ago, I was traveling in Europe speaking at several venues. My father had begun to travel with me. We arrived in Vienna, Austria, and were exhausted. We made our way up to our third-story flat and were pleasantly surprised at a spacious and clean environment. Looking around the room we spotted a mutual concern. There was one bed, and it was narrow, yet about ten feet long. We had much to do before bedtime, so we postponed the dilemma for later in the day.

We arrived back later in the evening and were quickly reminded of our challenge. We decided that the best method to rest was with each of our heads at opposite ends of the bed. Unfortunately, the bed was the exact size of us together, and our feet were touching in the middle! This presented a problem. We agreed to select a side of the narrow bed to claim as our own.

The night was a torturous one. All through the night, our feet would end up flat against each other's, waking us up. Apologies were expressed all night long until finally in the early morning, I awoke exhausted. Laying there in the early hours, I didn't have the strength to move my feet. So there they were, my feet and Dad's feet, foot to foot, heel to heel. I didn't realize it, but he was awake also.

The silence of the morning was interrupted by my father, calling out my name, "Stephan!" He began to declare a long word about my life. He prophetically framed words about what my future was to be. After he had called my name he said, "As my feet are, so your feet shall be." This became the theme of the unusual father-to-son encouragement. It was powerful. It was a defining moment for me. I realized in that moment how similar we were.

Any words spoken by my father would have had great impact, but the fact that his feet were touching my feet as he spoke, had an exponential effect! I didn't complain about the sleeping accommodations from that point on. Years later, looking back at that experience, I am astonished to track the accuracy of what he spoke and the memorable way in which it happened. My father is long gone, but I remember those words because of the unique demonstration.

VEHICLES OF GOD: ART

In recent years there has been an explosion of God's messages being communicated in or through the arts. One of the obvious examples would be the success of Mel Gibson's 2004 film, *The Passion of the Christ*. Under heavy controversy this relatively low-budget film swept across America. Many predicted it would fail.

After all, it was presented in an ancient language with English subtitles and was deemed narrow due to its religious message. Yet critics were silenced as this historic film generated hundreds of millions of dollars of revenue. The Gospel, according to Mel Gibson, had been preached with stunning results.

Stained glass was an early demonstration of art in the church. It depicted Bible stories to a mostly illiterate population. Through this art many were informed and inspired to know Christ and His ways. Sculpturing became another form of declaring the words of Heaven. Many churches today are recovering the value of all art forms and establishing art ministries out of their churches.

Poetry is when an emotion has found its thought and the thought has found words.

—Robert Frost (1874-1963)

I visited a church in Connecticut that exemplified this change. It was a large African-American church that put high value in prophetic art. Outstanding paintings were hanging throughout the building. A large, glass ceiling in the lobby spoke of the open heavens over the facility. A fountain springing in the lobby was a symbol of life for the thirsty. The pastor walked me through the process of how they built this prophetic structure and their belief in the power of symbolism. Everything in the church had prayerful thought behind it. The entire facility communicated. The message was one of hope and transforming power. Maybe that's why over 7,000 people attended there!

Messages Without Words

Saint Francis of Assisi is attributed as the author of this famous quote, "Preach the gospel always, and when necessary use words."[3] At Creation, God Himself used few words, yet demonstrated a visual that we still enjoy today. We are still discovering the extensive message in creation thousands of years later.

VEHICLES OF GOD: LIFE ITSELF

The greatest tool in God's hands is the human race itself. Each person is crafted and shaped through unique experiences, both bad and good. The Bible says that we are earthen vessels filled with a treasure. God the artist fashions us for His message. Every drug addict who is freed from their bondage becomes a testimony of Heaven's mercy. The expressions of gifting both great and small speak of a creative and diverse God. We become His message.

Periodically, God chooses someone to super-express His message. A biblical example of this is Job or Hosea. Job was a demonstration of someone who did not do wrong yet suffered and continued to maintain a good heart. In the end, it was all paid back to him—and doubled. His life serves as a constant reminder of how to respond when times are difficult.

Hosea's story is even more interesting. God asked Hosea to take a prostitute as a wife. Even when she left him and was having relations with other men, Hosea took her back. His story becomes a living picture of God's love for us. Even though we reject God, He is still there for us.

Someone once said that each of us who follow God may be the only Bibles that some people will ever read. It is likely that God is using more of us than we know. He might even be using us without our permission. He can speak through you without you ever opening your mouth.

Racetracks and Firewood

God demonstrated this to me several years ago. A neighbor came over to my house to take some photos of one of my daughters who was going to a school event. My neighbor was an amateur photographer and offered to record the moment. When he arrived at the door, I noticed that he had a tie on. I never remember seeing him with a tie, so I joked with him about it. He told me that he and his wife were going to the horse races and having dinner.

As he walked out the door, I yelled, "Hey, put something on number eight in the seventh!"

He waved back with disbelief.

Later at the races, he turned to his wife and said, "Hey, what was that horse that Steve wanted me to bet on?"

Looking through the program, they discovered that the horse's name was "Unshakable Faith." They told me later that upon looking through the entire program, that was the only horse with a religious name. They thought that this was strange. He informed me that he bet on it, and it lost. I quipped back, "Maybe there was another message in that!"

Later that week, I had a similar incident with another neighbor. I buy firewood every year and needed to order more for the winter. Months before, my neighbor had told me that if I ever needed wood pallets to let him know. He could get them for free. The pallets were great to stack the wood on and keep it dry. I walked out the door and crossed over my yard to ask him if he could bring me some in the next several weeks.

In response to my inquiry, he got a weird look on his face. I thought that I might have said something wrong. He asked me why I was asking him now. I let him know that I was ordering wood, but that there was no hurry. It turns out that as he left work that day, he sensed that he needed to bring some pallets home. It felt like one of those "Twilight Zone" moments. You know, the kind where you suspect that something supernatural or at least unusual is happening.

He then grinned wryly and said, "How many do you need?"

I honestly said, "Three."

Turning to get his coat, he replied with a shaking head, "Well, I have exactly three in my truck!"

I believe that this was not by accident. Without my knowledge, God was ministering something to the neighbor at the racetrack and the neighbor with the firewood pallets. Maybe He wanted them to know that they could hear from God also. I'm not sure, but I do believe that God was using my everyday life as an illustration to those around me. Don't be surprised if you are being watched...by God and those around you. Your life and actions are a voice from Heaven!

PASSENGERS IN THE VEHICLES: THE MESSAGE

Once I was sitting in the living room of a farmhouse studying. (It has since become one of my favorite places to study.) It was late spring, and I had been experiencing a series of personal and professional challenges. My heart was heavy. I began to pray one of those simple prayers that erupt out of a depleted heart: "Lord, help!"

I felt strangely narrowed into a prayer as I looked out on the cornfields that had been harvested the previous fall. The stalks had been cut down and had weathered the winter and looked beaten and defeated. My prayer of desperation came out, "Lord, end the winter and bring us spring." Immediately, my mind remembered a verse from an Old Testament passage:

For lo, the winter is past,
The rain is over and gone.
The flowers appear on the earth;
The time of singing has come,
And the voice of the turtledove
Is heard in our land (Song of Solomon 2:11-12).

In that exact moment, I heard a pecking noise coming from a back room. I began to slowly investigate, walking cautiously, not knowing its origins. Walking into a front bedroom, I noticed a robin pecking at the window as if trying to get in. Robins are a picture of the first sign of spring. Could this be an expression of Heaven? Does God use birds?

God uses many different means of revealing Himself and His message. That message can energize you in three different ways. It's like the *passenger* in God's vehicles. As mentioned earlier, His vehicles include dreams, impressions, visions, etc. The *passenger* brings the message to us by revelation, impartation, or inspiration.

The robin in the above story was a vehicle, a living parable that brought inspiration. Every expression from Heaven should have an effect on the person receiving it. The robin, combined with the Bible verse, brought a message that impacted me. I had been discouraged, but I was instantly transported to a place of hope and faith. A message from God will alter your circumstance. The appearance of the robin brought encouragement—strange vehicle, peculiar message, yet undeniable fruit. Consider the following diagram.

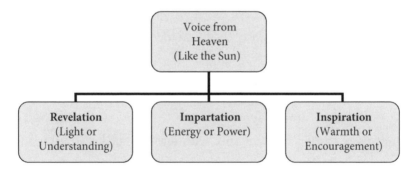

THE MESSAGE BRINGS REVELATION (LIGHT)

One of the ways that a message impacts us is in the same way that the Sun touches us. The rising of the Sun brings light and understanding to everything around us. Without it, we would wander in darkness. Actually, all of life would cease without the influence of our star known as the Sun. Heaven's message has a similar impact as the Sun. First of all, it turns the lights on, or enlightens. All of a sudden we have understanding where it wasn't easily seen before.

Hotel Lessons

I've stayed in many hotel rooms around the world. It's quite unsettling to get up in the middle of the night and not know where you are. Groping and grasping around an unfamiliar room can be scary and dangerous! Suddenly, your eyes adjust as a small sliver of light from under the door acts as a beacon of hope. Like a clearing fog, objects dimly reappear around the room.

When you finally turn the lights on, all things make sense. Boldness and clarity fill your heart. You know where you are and where you need to go. Many times all that is needed from Heaven is a bit of clarity.

Joseph, the father of Jesus, was like any other man. When he heard that his young wife was pregnant, knowing that he had no relations with her, he probably wondered what he should think or do. An angel spoke to him in a dream bringing sharp clarity and confirmation. The Bible says that when Joseph awakened, he did what the angel had spoken for him to do.

The Bible is replete with examples of God giving confirmation or revelation to help followers trust what He had spoken. Many words that come from Heaven are meant to illuminate. Our cities and nations need leaders who can find the light and bring its revelation to bear on the problems of our culture.

THE MESSAGE BRINGS IMPARTATION (ENERGY)

Again using the illustration of the Sun, we can see that a message from God imparts *energy*. Solar panels are increasing in popularity; they are used as collectors of the Sun's energy seek to convert its power into various uses. Heaven's words can also bring a literal energy to do a task.

The ancient prophet Elijah needed a fresh injection of spiritual strength. He had actually become so depressed that he asked God to let him die. In response, God sent an angel to feed him and give him a message. That message was converted into real energy, giving him strength for 40 days and nights. That's quite a meal and message! Something was imparted, which went beyond the natural, and brought supernatural strength.

Any good news seems to have this effect. The mood in a family or company can be changed by one good report. A well-placed word can blow away the winds of adversity. What do you think a message from Heaven might do?

Negative words will cause people to lose heart. Israel was held up from entering their promised land due to a bad report. The news of a few stopped an entire nation from entering their destiny. They immediately considered themselves small and the task too daunting. Bad words stopped them in their tracks. It literally robbed them of their energy.

In ancient times, in another situation, the Jews were commissioned to rebuild their temple. Discouragement had set in and they had ceased labor for 16 years. What words could possibly arouse these lethargic people? God raised up a prophet named Haggai to speak to them and exhort them. Several short paragraphs of challenge and the simple phrase, "*I am with you,*" was enough to stir their hearts (Hag. 1:13). It wasn't the words as much as it was the impartational power in the words. Words have the ability to bring supernatural energy. They immediately can squeeze lemons into lemonade. The Sun can be harnessed to provide energy and so can messages from Heaven. Some words from Heaven will produce action, like the impact of wind on a windmill or Sun on a solar panel—energy is harnessed and positive action occurs as a result.

Word Energy Throughout History

History is packed with examples of men and women who spoke words that must have originated from Heaven. The words may not have been extraordinary, yet they had an imparting effect to calm or energize a nation. Winston Churchill made a number of speeches that fit in this category. His 1940 speech, "We Shall Fight on the Beaches," and his 1941 speech entitled, "Never Give In!" stirred his nation and the world in trying times of world war. It gave war-weary people a framework of hope to hold onto.

President George W. Bush struck a similar chord in his "Bullhorn" speech of 2001. Standing on the rubble of the terrorist-devastated World Trade Center, he grabbed a bullhorn and said to a cheering crowd, "I can hear you. The rest of the world hears you. And the people who knocked down these buildings will hear all of us soon."[4]

Energized chants from the crowd erupted shouting, "USA! USA!" His words were the type of words that inspire a nation in a time of great need. I believe that many of these historic words are not merely clever or timely, but Heaven-sent.

One of the most spectacular stories in the Bible involves the prophet Ezekiel speaking over a valley of dry bones. His words, when energized by Heaven, had the power to bring life in the driest of situations. His Heaven-sent words manifested in the array of a mighty army. Heaven's words can truly impart energy for the soul.

Feeling sorry for yourself, and your present condition, is not only a waste of energy but the worst habit you could possibly have.

—Dale Carnegie (1888-1955)

THE MESSAGE BRINGS INSPIRATION (WARMTH)

The simplest result from Heaven's words is encouragement. This might appear to be weak or unimportant, yet most of the time all we need is simple encouragement. I believe that most encouraging words originate in Heaven and are part of the seed that is in each one of us. We were created in God's image and therefore speak as He might speak.

A "Well done" or an "Atta boy" from a coach, teacher, or parent is enough to quench a thirsty soul. God is an encourager and wants to praise the smallest of progress. After all, isn't that even in the nature of true fathers? A good father will encourage a child in things that are very small. One small step. Ten feet on a bicycle alone. Eating a meal on our own. All of these are opportunities for simple praise. It's in the nature of God, and it has been placed in every human being. Encouragement is a good thing, even more when it is directly ordered by God. It begins a transformation.

THE DESTINATION: TRANSFORMATION AND ACTIVATION

Someone once said that Heaven's words are to "build up, lift up, and cheer up, that we might grow up!" God is interested in fruit, growth, and maturity. The voice from Heaven does not speak without intention. It's all about change, transformation, and activation into a productive and fruitful life. It would be wasted energy from Heaven for us to hear only and not do. The Bible gives constant warnings to those who hear yet are not changed. In fact, several of Jesus' parables are dedicated to this subject.

Jesus likens the person who only *hears* to someone who has built their house on sand (Matt. 7:26). These people who are given to listening to many words, yet do not obey and change, will ultimately collapse under the trial of the day. The wind and the waves of life will come and great will be their fall. On the other hand, if you listen and obey, you are compared to a house built on a rock, and thus can withstand the storms of life.

This is the scary part about hearing from God. You are now responsible to do what He tells you to do!

> *...receive with meekness the implanted word, which is able to save your souls. But be doers of the word, and not hearers only, deceiving yourselves* (James 1:21-22).

THE GOAL IS TRANSFORMATION

The ultimate goal of a voice from Heaven is your transformation. It will move us from being an unproductive, lethargic, self-serving people into vibrant, joy-filled individuals. This is the destination that is planned for us all: being conformed into the nature of God Himself. Obedience to His voice is the greatest vehicle for change. Begin to put your ear to the ground—or actually to the sky. He's speaking for your good!

EXPLORING THE VOICE QUESTIONS:

1. Have there been any other vehicles besides the ones mentioned that God has used to bring a message to you?

2. What other historical figures have been used of God to communicate a message? How?

3. When has a word from Heaven rescued you or set you back on the right path?

DO IT YOURSELF!

Ask someone to allow you to pray over them. Speak an audible prayer and allow God to "pepper" it with Heaven's understanding. He will take you deeper and give you revelation to unlock and heal hearts.

Endnotes

1. Jill Neimark, "Night Life—Dreams," *Psychology Today* (July/August 1998).

2. http://usinfo.state.gov/usa/infousa/facts/democrac/38.htm.

3. Ihttp://www.livingcatholicism.com/archives/2005/04/ simple_ways_to.html.

4. George W. Bush's "Bullhorn" speech can be heard on the Internet at: http://www.archive.org/details/GeorgeBushBullhornSpeech AtGroundZero_9_14_2001.

Chapter Four

UNLOCKING THE VOICE:

The Key to
Opening the Download from Heaven

Do not forget to entertain strangers, for by so doing some have unwittingly entertained angels (Hebrews 13:2).

I was in Florida on vacation, and I had just gathered my children together after a refreshing meal at a local restaurant. That was back when our children were young and any family event at a public place was a challenge. We kept our young ones entertained with little bags of crackers. They made a mess, but they're worth their weight in gold. Peace reigns when crackers are in hand!

My wife and I had cleaned up the table as best we could, paid the bill, and headed out into the parking lot. It was a beautiful Florida evening, and we didn't have a care in the world as we strolled toward the car. Suddenly, someone began yelling from back at the restaurant. I turned to note that it was our waitress, and she was yelling at me!

I was startled to say the least and made my way back to the door to see what was bothering her. It turns out that she was yelling at me because I had not left a tip. My children had made a mess and we hadn't compensated her for the trouble. She also noticed by our license plate that we were from Canada and made a few comments about not coming back again.

In some strange way, this might be justified except that I had left her a generous tip, but it was on the credit card. When I corrected the misunderstanding, she said, "Well, I'm sorry," and returned to her duties. Unfortunately, we were now all frazzled by this robust confrontation, and I went in to talk to the owner. Needless to say, he was not pleased and bathed us with apologies.

I think of this incident often, even though it happened many years ago. Waitresses and waiters are people who serve, speak kindly, and are rewarded through tips. I understand that it is a thankless job and no doubt they receive much abuse. However, I wish to point out that this is an absolute picture of how our attitudes will unlock potential favor or opportunity that wouldn't have otherwise been opened.

My waitress became angry because she thought she had been overlooked, when in fact the reward simply came in a different fashion than she had expected. Do you remember the old saying, "When God closes a door, He opens a window"? Well, that's true in the mathematics of Heaven. We sow our service into Heaven and, often without knowing it, reap the harvest (blessing) in many other ways. I might not be able to see the fruit immediately, but nevertheless, it's hidden there somewhere.

It's easy to get frustrated when we have served, and yet it appears that our voice and our actions have not been seen or heard. They *have*—at least by Heaven. The tip may be on the card instead of on the table!

A merchant who approaches business with the idea of serving the public well has nothing to fear from the competition.

—*James Cash Penney (1875-1971)*

A friendly bartender in Kansas found this principle to be true. Cindy Kienow had been working at an Applebee's restaurant for eight years, and the largest tip she had ever received was $230. According to a CBS news report on September 1, 2006, a regular visiting customer paid his $26 bill and left Cindy a $10,000 tip! She said, "We were just talking and having fun, and then he just ate and ran his card and wrote it down for me." Cindy was shocked and speechless.

The customer told her that she deserves it and that she should buy something nice with the money.[1] Simply serving and demonstrating hospitality opened a small treasure for Kienow. It may open a treasure for you also. Heaven responds to a serving heart.

SERVING'S SECRETS

Serving can be a key that unlocks a destiny, which may come in a package that we aren't used to nor do we expect. The Bible refers to this truth, cautioning us that our service may open the door for a message from Heaven (angels or messengers).

Let brotherly love continue. Do not forget to entertain strangers, for by so doing some have unwittingly entertained angels (Hebrews 13:1-2).

You never know, but the people you serve, work for, or are related too, may have a message for you that originates in Heaven. That obviously cannot be our motivation for service, but it is a great, fringe benefit!

Recently, I was diagnosed with a serious physical problem. There is no conventional treatment recommended at this time. Many people have suggested alternative therapies, which we have checked into. One man suggested that I visit a nutrition-oriented therapy clinic approximately one hour away from where I live. I went to the clinic, and it seemed to be the choice that I would want to make. The problem? One month of treatment cost $10,000.

The head of the clinic informed me that the cost had been covered by a man I barely knew. It turns out that he had attended some conferences that I have put on and had benefited from them. He had secretly helped numerous people with different life challenges. I didn't realize that one of the solutions to my dilemma was already in my life...I had entertained an angel! Perhaps not a real angel, but pretty close.

In the time of Jesus Christ, Israel had no idea that the One whom they had sought for thousands of years was already in their city, walking down their streets. It took spiritual eyes and ears to discern the solution at their door. Only a few did. Many missed the living message that was already in their neighborhood.

There is a story of Abraham in the Bible that is related to this. Abraham was very old and had just had surgery...circumcision (see Gen. 17). The text in the very next chapter states that he was sitting in the tent door in the heat of the day. He was probably recovering. That's major surgery for a 99-year-old man! I'm sure he didn't feel like serving anyone. Even in this state though, he jumped up to help the visitors—who were actually holding a verbal key to his destiny. He was, of course, unaware of this at the time. This is what makes the story so magnificent!

Three men—who are later identified as angels—stopped by. Apparently they were on their way to destroy Sodom and Gomorrah. Abraham shows typical desert hospitality, hastening to make the best of meals for his guests. He then waits nearby to see if they have any additional needs.

They proceeded to predict specifics about his future. One of the most profound and specific words that Abraham had ever heard came in an atmosphere of serving. The angels promised him that he would have a son in his old age. You never know how the reward of your service will be returned to you.

SOWING AND WEEPING

In January 2005, America began the first day of having its first black, female Secretary of State: Condoleezza Rice. She was greeted at the State Department with employees lined up clapping and welcoming her. She made her way to a makeshift stage to give a welcome and pep talk to the employees.

Rice commented that her first government job was as an intern at the State Department many years before. That comment probably made some old-timers in the State Department nervous. Some of the people who had been her bosses when she was just an intern were still working there. Imagine the thoughts that might have ran through their heads: *Is she that young black girl who I gave a hard time?* In her public greeting she jokingly said, "Now, there's a lesson in that: Be good to your interns."[2]

The nine most terrifying words in the English language are, "I'm from the government and I'm here to help."

—Ronald Reagan (1911-2004)

When I heard that speech, I thought, *Wow, you never know who is around you and how they may be a part of your destiny.* I'm sure that some State Department employees might have been considering early retirement on that day! It pays to be a servant to those around you. They may be the carriers of a message from Heaven or may play a vital role in your future or destiny. I tell everyone to be kind to children: They may be your heart surgeon someday!

CAMEL KINDNESS

A classic romance story in the Bible describes this idea of being a *carrier* of hidden destiny. Abraham commissioned his servant to find a wife for his son, Isaac. The servant loaded down ten camels with riches that are assumed to be a settlement for the new wife. He arrived at a city and had his camels kneel down by a well. Wells were apparently a great place to find women in those days!

The servant prayed a simple prayer, as follows:

Behold, here I stand by the well of water, and the daughters of the men of the city are coming out to draw water. Now let it be that the young woman to whom I say, "Please let down your pitcher that I may drink," and she says, "Drink, and I will also give your camels a drink"—let her be the one You have appointed for Your servant Isaac. And by this I will know that You have shown kindness to my master" (Genesis 24:13-14).

I know…it's a strange way to find a mate, but that's how it was done in this case.

Sure enough, as soon as he finished his prayer, a woman who was *"very beautiful to behold"* came to the well (Gen. 24:16). In biblical terms, this was one "hot" woman. The servant then went through the motions and asked her if he could have a drink. This appears to be a test of the woman's heart. Is she a servant? Does she know how to consider even the stranger?

She passed the test with flying colors. Not only does she give him a drink, but she fulfilled the prophetic prayer and moves to water the camels also. The Bible says that she "quickly" drew water and "ran" back to the well. This woman had a servant's heart and was eager to serve. What she didn't realize was that she was watering her future destiny...on the back of some smelly camel.

She had no idea that the camels and their contents were going to be gifts to her. It didn't matter. Her motive was pure. I imagine that as she was giving water to the camels and noticing that they were laden down with many riches, she might have wondered, "Somebody's got some money!" Maybe she realized that it was destined as a gift for a bride and thought, *What a blessed woman it is who will receive this great treasure!* Little did she know that the eyes of the servant were watching her. Maybe God is watching us, looking for the servant's heart.

Soon it was revealed to her that she was to be the recipient of the great gift. After a night of meeting the family, Rebekah climbed upon the camels and proceeded toward a storybook ending. She was willing to serve, not knowing that a messenger was present who would alter her life. It is the right thing to do—especially for a person attempting to hear from God—to serve. Serving becomes a key that will eventually become a *Master* key, opening many doors that might have never been otherwise manifested.

Maybe it would be appropriate at this time to ask you, "Whose camels are you watering?" Someone around you may be holding that key. Serving another's vision can open your own vision. Some smelly environment might hold your future. We have little clue about who God has placed around us and the impact that they are purposed to have.

SURPRISE TRAVEL COMPANION

Two men were walking with Jesus one day. The thing that makes this story unusual is that they did not know that it was Jesus. After all, He had just been killed! Walking along, they were fascinated at this stranger and His knowledge of all things. The Bible says that *"Beginning at Moses and all the Prophets, He expounded to them in all the Scriptures the things concerning Himself"* (Luke 24:27). I'd love to have a recording of that conversation!

We aren't sure why they didn't know who He was. They knew about Him and had placed great hopes in His ability to save Israel. They were somehow closely associated with the company of people who had been with Jesus and who had arrived at the tomb after His resurrection. They were possibly "second tier" disciples of Christ, but were restrained from recognizing who He actually was.

Something happened though…as it always does. They implored the guest to come in and have supper with them. They were showing hospitality to a stranger. As they sat down to eat with this intriguing man, they had an epiphany. Suddenly their eyes were opened and they had understanding as to whom they had been traveling with…Jesus Himself! You want to talk about missing a moment! Imagine what went through their minds, *What was that joke I told Him on the road?*

I'm sure the greatest regret was, "Why didn't we see who He really was?" In fact, their comment to the others was, *"Did not our heart burn within us while He talked with us on the road, and while He opened the Scriptures to us?"* (Luke 24:32). They realized after the fact that they had experienced internal signs that were trying to communicate to them who this person actually was.

Hints and road signs are present in every encounter, as Heaven tries to deliver an understanding of who you are actually with and what is really happening! Had these two men not invited the stranger in, they may have never found the secret of the moment. What a story they now had to tell the guys at work!

LITTLE PACKAGES

Bill Gates is the richest man in the world. He dropped out of college to pursue his dream. An Internet site called thinkquest.org describes his early years: "His overly talkative and extremely sarcastic personality worried his parents, who later sent him to a psychiatrist."[3]

Little did anyone know that this man had camels heavy with treasure that had not yet been revealed. His personality was hiding one of history's most extraordinary talents. I'm sure that there were many acquaintances in Bill's past who now wish that they had been more gracious and patient with him.

Bill Gates took many people with him on his journey, including his good friend, Paul Allen (co-founder of Microsoft), and Harvard buddy, Steve Ballmer. Actually, their lives were intertwined with shared destiny. They needed each other and respected and benefited from each relationship. No journey is accomplished alone! They discovered their God-given destinies when involved in helping one another.

CRACKED POTS

Every time circumstances have "wonder" attached to them, I'm suspicious. Does God have something unusual hidden in this encounter? Messengers from Heaven are all around us. They may not even know that they are being used by God! For example, somebody in Jerusalem owned an ordinary donkey that was used to escort Jesus into His purpose. God loves to catapult the ordinary into the extraordinary!

I love the fact that God chooses *"earthen vessels"* (2 Cor. 4:7) to store His treasures. We're all just cracked pots, containing something that has been sought after for centuries: the mystery of the ages. Don't consider anything to be chance. There might be gold hidden in those barren hills of relationship!

Friends and family hold keys. Children and strangers may contain a message that will impact your life. Circumstances might reveal a parable that brings you hope in a time of need.

MOTORCYCLE PARABLES

This past summer, I was riding my motorcycle with my brother. We had ridden all day and were turning toward home. I was cruising down a secondary road when I noticed a car about to pull onto the road I was traveling on. I made eye contact with the driver and assumed that he saw me. He didn't.

I approached at about 45 miles per hour when all of a sudden he pulled out in front of me and stopped. I stood on the brakes and went into a 60-foot skid. My mind was racing in a moment of survival. I decided in milliseconds to lay down my bike, skidding into the side of the vehicle. I lay on the pavement stunned, trying to remove a 600-pound motorcycle off of my leg. My brother came to my rescue, and miraculously, I was not injured.

The police arrived and cited the driver. Paramedics checked me and released me. My motorcycle had sustained some minor scrapes, but was in surprisingly great condition. I mounted the bike and went home. I now recognize that event as a parable in my life. It had a message that prepared me for devastating news that I was about to receive.

The shock of the "near death" experience had an interesting effect on me. I cried without warning for several days after. My heart was being plowed and tenderized for a purpose. God was having mercy on me and my emotions.

Two weeks later, I had a surgery that my doctor had recommended for closer investigation of a lump under my arm. Five days later, I discovered that I had a serious condition. The first several days were difficult. "Incurable" is a powerful word. I assumed my life was over. It wasn't. It turned out to be a situation that doesn't require treatment at this time.

In those early days, as I was contemplating my unusual summer, I received understanding. I understood that my motorcycle accident had a message in it. The interpretation was: Even though I would be stopped in my tracks, others would be there to help me up. What appeared fatal was only a frightening stop in the road of life.

The insurance company had paid me over $3,000 for the few scratches on my bike. I believed that the evil force that tried to rob me of life would also be made to compensate. Whoever I was prior to the diagnosis was changed. The resolve in me has transformed to a desire to help others. It's payback time. My life is dedicated to removing fear and building confidence that Heaven has a plan, and it must happen.

It is quite possible that all around you exists the framework of your assignment from Heaven. If you keep the heart of a servant and listen closely to the indicators of life, you might possibly unravel this mystery that perplexes many: "What is my purpose?"

Rick Warren's book, *The Purpose-Driven Life,* did not become the best-selling hardback book in American history by accident. Over 30 million copies sold to a hungry population who have spent their lives searching…for the key…to unlock the treasure that is within. Again I ask, "Whose camels are you watering?"

Exploring the Voice Questions:

1. Have you ever entertained an angel? Tell the story of how someone helped you in an extraordinary situation. Have you been someone else's "angel"?

2. What are ways to combine serving and the giving of words from Heaven?

3. Who has God brought into your life for you to serve? How might you be a carrier of treasure for them?

Do It Yourself!

Speak a blessing over someone. Speak good words from your heart and allow God to enhance them with knowledge from Heaven.

Endnotes

1. "Kansas Bartender Gets $10,000 Tip," accessed on the Internet at: http://www.cbsnews.com/stories/2006/09/01/earlyshow/main1959975.shtml.

2. Secretary Condoleezza Rice, "Welcome Remarks to Employees," Jan. 27, 2005. Information retrieved on the Internet at: http://www.state.gov/secretary/rm/2005/41261.htm.

3. Information retrieved on the Internet at: http://library.thinkquest.org/C0115420/Cyber-club%20800x600/BIO/Bill%20Gates.htm.

Chapter Five

INTENSITY OF THE VOICE:

Learning the

Tone of Heaven's Communication

…His voice as the sound of many waters (Revelation 1:15).

T HERE are many ways to communicate. The intensity of our communication is another entire layer of how we relate. Research done by Professor Albert Mehrabian at UCLA indicates that some of the greater communication is actually nonverbal. In the article, "Six Reasons to Improve Your Body Language," Mehrabian is quoted as saying that "words are only 7 percent of your communication."[1] This eye-opening article causes one to pause and think. Communication is so much more complicated than we realize.

After 29 years of marriage, I totally understand what is being expressed in this article. I can be at a party, and one look from my wife says volumes. I know without conversing with her when it's time to go home. We have actually carried on conversations without talking. Later, in a safe place we laughingly remember…

"I knew exactly what you were thinking!" Words are only one part of relating and evidently a small part at that.

Communication also includes a person's tonality, which accounts for 38 percent, and body language, 55 percent. Can you imagine that the tone of what you say accounts for more than what you actually say! All my mother had to do was raise her voice, and the quantity and quality of the message changed exponentially.

Heaven's voice will come with varied intensity also. It takes time to discern the level. Have we not seen this dynamic in raising our families? When I ask my kids to do something, I usually begin in soft tones. If no response comes, my tone may become more animated.

If I was near one of my children and they were in danger, a shout of warning might not suffice. Bodily interference might have to take place.

When my son was a toddler, he accidentally stepped into the deep end of a pool. My wife instinctively reached in and grabbed him before his entire body even got wet. Her communication had to be on a different level. You do what needs to be done to get the message across.

Whispering is appropriate intensity when someone is close by and their attention is focused on you. Lifting your voice and the using gestures might help to get attention in other circumstances. God functions in a similar way. Look at the following chart to see the seven levels of intensity.

This diagram represents different intensities in which God deals with humans. Understand that this is not a complete picture,

INTENSITY COMMUNICATION CYCLES

Visitation Elevation

Sensation Transportation **Ebb & Flow**

Evacuation

Impression

Disconnection

but represents the infinite number of nuances that God uses to communicate with us. The gray center represents the "God realm." This is the place where His voice is heard or felt.

IMPRESSION

Let's look a little closer at each of the types of intensities as shown on the previous diagram. *Impression* is that gentle, still voice that we hear in our heart. Elijah was tutored by God to hear Him in the "*still small voice.*"

Then He said, "Go out, and stand on the mountain before the Lord." And behold, the Lord passed by, and a great and strong wind tore into the mountains and broke the rocks in pieces before the Lord, but the Lord was not in the wind; and after the wind an earthquake, but the Lord was not in the earthquake; and after the earthquake a fire, but the Lord was not in the fire; and after the fire a still small voice (1 Kings 19:11-12).

God was in the small voice. I've covered this in more detail in another part of the book. It's the kiss of God. It's the flutter of feeling that comes when God is quietly speaking. Most of what you hear from Heaven will fall into this category. It's important to become familiar with the sound of Heaven's voice to you!

An impression is that place that barely brushes against the voice of God. It may feel like a soft whisper, yet leaves you with a deep sense that God has spoken.

It's that same sense that is given to you to discern when people have been talking about you. I'm not referring to paranoia, but that uncanny sense when you walk into a room that you are either being received or rejected. Nobody has to say anything. It's just there. You hear it. It's that same sense that causes someone to stand out in the crowd, even though you have no reason to notice them.

I've found that, many times, coincidences and odd happenings are God's communication through environments into my spirit. I pay attention now. The impression is the tool God uses most to get my attention. It's still and gentle, but powerful in your heart.

SENSATION

The next area of intensity is *Sensation*. This is beyond the impression, and has actual physical confirmation that God is communicating. The famous English preacher, John Wesley, reported upon conversion that his heart was "strangely warmed." History is replete with examples of individuals who felt the presence of God or the voice of Heaven.

The New Testament account in the Book of Acts records a fantastic sensation on the Jewish holiday of Pentecost. The disciples were gathered with others when they heard a *"sound from Heaven as of a rushing mighty wind"* (Acts 2:2). This takes the experience to an entirely new level. The disciples were not moving on a mere imagination of God, but a tangible, audible, and even visible manifestation of Heaven's presence. They see something that they described as *"divided tongues"* (Acts 2:3) on the heads of their companions. The author, Luke, describes them as being *"filled"* and full of utterance (Acts 2:4).

This one encounter experienced by 120 people and witnessed by thousands of onlookers has the fruit of great boldness that forced others to judge them as drunk. In one moment, their ears, eyes, bodies, and mouths were impacted by the sound of Heaven. Contemporary examples of this type of sensation would include shaking, tingling, warmth, and more.

I suppose that this would stand to reason. If you stick your finger in a light socket, you will have sensation! How much more if you get in touch with the foundation of the universe! Something just might happen. Although many would argue that we shouldn't look for manifestation of God, I believe it is reasonable to have expectation when talking to Him. Should He be the only being in the universe who does not carry on a normal conversation? There will be times in your life, if you pursue Heaven, that you will be fully aware of His presence.

VISITATION

The audience grows smaller as we explore the deeper intensifications of God. The next level goes beyond sensation into *Visitation*. Throughout the Bible, visitation came especially at key moments. In Acts chapter 12 the apostle Peter was in prison, presumably about to be executed. An angel stood by him, and a light shined around him. Peter had been chained between two soldiers, and guards were at the door. Supernaturally, in this visitation, Peter is freed to return to his friends. This realm involves the encountering of other entities...mainly non-human.

Practically every famous Old Testament character had a visitation by God. Noah was told to prepare an ark. Abraham was told to leave his country. Prophets were instructed in different ways by open-eyed visitations. In the New Testament, Stephen saw the heavens open with Jesus standing at the right hand of God. Paul was struck down off of his high horse and rebuked by a voice, which identified itself as Jesus. Almost every player in the nativity story had visitations. The wise men, shepherds, Mary and Joseph all had visitations with clear instructions.

There was a 1907 spiritual revival called the "Azusa Street Revival," which was named after the street address of the magnificent heavenly download. It began in Los Angeles with a few poor people and soon spread all over the world, returning reports of extraordinary encounters. Frank Bartleman, a journalist, gave eyewitness reports in his book, *Azusa Street.* Strange visitations and accounts of supernatural communication began to proliferate.

In India, reports came back of "pictures appearing on the walls to a company of small girls in prayer, supernaturally depicting the life of Christ." In Wales, "Colored lights were often seen, like balls of fire during the revival there."[2] This stretch for our thinking doesn't seem to hinder God, who says:

> *"For My thoughts are not your thoughts, nor are your ways My ways," says the Lord. "For as the heavens are higher than the earth, so are My ways higher than your ways, and My thoughts than your thoughts"* (Isaiah 55:8-9).

ELEVATION

This is where things get crazy. It gets a little more difficult for the Western-trained mind to function when you start messing with the human position. We've all heard stories of hitchhikers whom we thought might be an angel, and we've watched television shows that depict this supernatural possibility. Even those who do not believe in Heaven seem to allow room for a realm that is *other-worldly* and not fully understood.

It's when you begin to look at the concept of *Elevation* that skeptics quickly move in. This is the idea that God would come and literally pick someone up and possibly take them into a heavenly place.

Parents are sometimes forced to use this level of intensity. If you have a young child that is playing in an area that is a threat to them, you might say, "Don't touch!" Now we all know that such parental admonishments are met with multiple challenges, the biggest being the word "No!" We might raise our voice, but if the danger is great enough we will communicate by literally removing the child from the vicinity. Or, for example, an approaching dog might startle a child and force parents to lift them up out of harm's way. We may also lift a young child to help them get a better perspective, such as at a ball game.

There are several instances in Scripture that record the lifting of an individual in order to communicate something. It cannot be ignored! The prophet Ezekiel was sitting by the river Chebar, when *"the heavens were opened,"* and he *"saw visions of God"* (Ezek. 1:1). I think that this would be enough of an experience to speak whatever God wanted to speak, yet He takes it to another level…literally!

Ezekiel witnesses the processes of Heaven in magnificent visions. God speaks a strong word to him to go to the captives. Then it happens:

> *Then the Spirit lifted me up, and I heard behind me a great thunderous voice: "Blessed is the glory of the Lord from His place!"* (Ezekiel 3:12).

This unusual occurrence happens several times. In fact, at one time in Ezekiel 8:3, he is lifted up by *"a lock of his hair"*!

Apparently this type of communication is not confined just to Old Testament prophets. Evan Roberts, a leading participant in the Welsh revival of the early 1900s reported, "One Friday night last spring, while praying by my bedside before retiring, I was taken up to a great expanse, without time or space. It was communion with God. Before this I had had a far off God. I was frightened that night, but never since."[3] This once-in-a-lifetime experience began to occur every night for three months!

The apostle Paul had a similar experience. It was so inexpressible that he wrestled with how it actually happened.

> *It is doubtless not profitable for me to boast. I will come to visions and revelations of the Lord: I know a man in Christ who fourteen years ago—whether in the body I do not know, or whether out of the body I do not know, God knows—such a one was caught up to the third heaven. And I know such a man—whether in the body or out of the body I do not know, God knows—how he was caught up into Paradise and heard inexpressible words, which it is not lawful for a man to utter* (2 Corinthians 12:1-4).

This elevation-type occurrence, although not common, seems to be key in turning the heart of an individual whom God is recruiting for an extraordinary task. The Bible gives no reference that Isaiah was "caught up," yet he experiences much of what the others saw in similar situations. In Isaiah chapter 6, he describes a throne room, and God gives him a call that apparently needed a supernatural imprint.

The Revelation of Jesus Christ, which was written by John, contains a strange invitation. John, the closest friend of Jesus, had been exiled to an island called Patmos. There he experienced a complex series of visions and communications that continue to baffle many today.

In chapter 4 of Revelation, a door in Heaven stands open and a voice like a trumpet says, *"Come up here, and I will show you things..."* (Rev. 4:1). What an invitation! Immediately, he was *"in the Spirit"* and began to see a throne room (Rev. 4:2). Although, the text does not say that he was elevated, it is implied. Think about it: One moment he is looking at a door, being invited to come up, and the next minute he is in a throne room. He was elevated.

This type of intensity of communication seems to be reserved for extraordinary commissioning or revelations. It's a lifting up, to see something from His perspective. Those who experience it are never the same.

TRANSPORTATION

Ah...yes...the *Transportation* of humans for Heaven's purposes. This intensity not only involves the touching and lifting of a human, but the change of geography. Sometimes God needs to get you somewhere quickly. Our prophetic buddy, Ezekiel, appears once again for our consideration. In Ezekiel 3:14, Ezekiel says that *"the Spirit lifted me up and took me away, and I went in bitterness, in the heat of my spirit."* He doesn't sound like a willing participant! He is apparently hesitant, possibly falling into the same category as Moses and Jonah. (These were two other individuals for whom God had to use extreme measures to soften them for the task.)

Ezekiel is so shaken by the experience that he sits without speaking, "*astonished*" or "*overwhelmed*" (NIV), for seven days (Ezek. 3:15). I can't say that I blame him! After all, he was transported directly to the people he was called to speak to. At least these ancient prophets saved on travel expenses!

The Book of Acts records a story regarding an ordinary man named Philip. Philip had been appointed to serve tables in Jerusalem but liked to dabble in the extraordinary on the side. He was on a roll. He had seen great miracles, even the healing of paralytics and the lame. Not bad for a mere servant! Reinforcements were called in to take it to a new level, and in humble fashion, Philip moves on, being led by the voice of God (see Acts 8:6,26).

Philip encounters an African with great authority. He is known in the Bible as the Ethiopian Eunuch. This was a divine appointment. It was one of those right-place-at-the-right-time circumstances.

Philip gives revelation to the seeker, baptizes him in water, and moves to his next God assignment. His means of transportation to this next assignment is what remains curious. Most commentators on this verse either ignore it or continue in the passage as if nothing has happened. One well-known commentator, F.F. Bruce says, "he was sped northwards by the Spirit on another mission."[4]

Now when they came up out of the water, the Spirit of the Lord caught Philip away, so that the eunuch saw him no more.... But Philip was found at Azotus (Acts 8:39-40).

Somehow Philip was *"seen no more"* by the Ethiopian but was transported 20 miles to Azotus, and without missing a beat, he keeps on preaching. The writer of Acts, Luke, doesn't seem to have a need to explain any further. Philip was in one place and was needed in another, so he was transported.

Apparently, the Old Testament prophet Elijah had a reputation for this kind of transporting. Elijah met a servant of King Ahab on the road and exhorted the servant to tell the king that he was present. The servant responds by saying, *"As soon as I am gone from you...the Spirit of the Lord will carry you to a place I do not know"* (1 Kings 18:12).

Again, traveling prophets questioned Elisha about the location of his mentor, Elijah. Wondering where he had disappeared to, they said, *"Please let them go and search for your master, lest perhaps the Spirit of the Lord has taken him up and cast him upon some mountain or into some valley"* (2 Kings 2:16).

Now that's an interesting reputation to have. Imagine having groups of people suspect that you have been transported by God to another location. It is clear that our understanding of God and His ways are limited. He can do what He wants to do, with whom He wants to do it, and at the time He chooses to do it!

EVACUATION

This intensity makes me think of rescue. I remember the great devastation of New Orleans in 2005. Hurricane Katrina hit that vibrant, American city, flooding its streets with great devastation. The television reports in the days following showed boats going door to door looking for survivors. Many extraordinary videos showed rescues from rooftops. Great controversy followed regarding the evacuation of citizens. A lot of time and money have been spent on studying that disaster to better serve cities in knowing how to move people quickly from a threatened location.

I have been in many cities in the world where there were streets signs instructing the safe and rapid removal of people in an emergency. Holland has signs to assist you in case the dikes collapse. Florida has hurricane routes. *Evacuation* is "the quick and safe removal of a person from a location."

There are two biblical accounts of the most intense communication one might have with God. It's when He totally removes you from planet Earth.

The first account is veiled in mystery and is located in the first book of the Bible, Genesis. The man involved was named Enoch, and he had a long life with sons and daughters. One verse speaks of his evacuation. The Bible says, *"And Enoch walked with God; and he was not, for God took him"* (Gen. 5:24). What? What does that mean? I have some questions! Unfortunately, the Bible remains silent on this unusual transition from the earthly realm into another.

The New Testament writer of Hebrews expands on the subject slightly. It is said of Enoch that he *"was taken away so that he did not see death, 'and was not found, because God had taken him'; for before he was taken he had this testimony, that he pleased God"* (Heb. 11:5). God must have *really* been pleased! Some people have speculated that Enoch walked with God daily, like Adam did in the garden; then one day as they were walking and talking, God said, "Hey, we're closer to My house than yours...why don't you come over!" Interesting thought. As you can see, this doesn't happen often but must be noted.

Elijah is the final character that we must look at in regards to evacuation. Songwriters have written songs about this story, and many people are familiar with it even if they never attended a church. It's a culturally-popular story that brings people hope in situations with no way out.

The popular, spiritual folk song, "Swing Low, Sweet Chariot" was written by Wallace Willis, a former slave.[5] Many have speculated over the years that this spiritual song was referring to the Underground Railroad, an escape route for American slaves seeking freedom. Regardless of whether that's true or not, it represented deliverance from bondage and escape to a better place. One thing we know for sure, it was referring to the Bible story of Elijah.

Elijah was a great prophet of the Old Testament whose ministry was accompanied by great signs and wonders. He was given to fear and depression at one point, yet continued to perform great feats of faith in his generation. Toward the end of his ministry he selected an assistant: Elisha. Elisha became an eyewitness to this evacuation account.

The two associates were walking and talking when all of a sudden, "*A chariot of fire appeared with horses of fire, and separated the two of them; and Elijah went up by a whirlwind into heaven*" (2 Kings 2:11). The New Testament portrays Elijah as a man with a "*nature like ours*" (James 5:17), yet indeed he lived a fruitful life.

Again, little explanation comes. The reader is left to wonder what makes God move in such an intensity of communication. I realize that all of us would like to be evacuated at one time or another in our lives. God in His infinite wisdom has apparently only chosen to do it twice!

DISCONNECTION

The final area of *intensity of communication* actually deals with one of the most powerful forms of all: silence. Does God communicate using silence? This disconnection is sometimes referred to as a "wilderness." A *wilderness* is "a place of separation and aloneness." Before we talk about the God aspect, let's first consider human relations.

If you pose a question to a friend and that friend does not answer, it may mean many things. Here are some possibilities:

1. Time is needed to weigh the full ramifications before answering.

2. You may not be prepared for the answer. It may not be what you want to hear and wrong action may result.

3. Time might be given for you to consider the validity of what has been asked...possibly answering your own question.

4. Silence can communicate the "awe" of the moment. Sometimes the moment shouldn't be disrupted by mere words.

5. Silence can indicate deep emotion, the inability to speak due to the emotional content or atmosphere.

I'm sure that there are many other reasons that can be explored in books or in studies on the Internet. My point is that sometimes silence is valid, and it can be a great communication tool. It can also be used as a weapon of manipulation. A passive-aggressive person can speak volumes through silence to produce fear and insecurity.

As we must account for every idle word, so must we account for every idle silence.

—Benjamin Franklin (1706-1790)

God is silent at times for His reasons. It never has to do with a lack of love for us, but rather a dire need to communicate. We must always function with our attitude and understanding toward God that He loves us. He doesn't tease us, manipulate us, or leave us without an ultimate revelation. We can discover the mystery of His silence, as we explore the depths of who He is.

The wilderness can be a punitive place or a place of development. In the story of Israel and their trek to the Promised Land, God took them through the wilderness on purpose. He wanted to strengthen them. In fact, the Bible says that if they went the easy way the people might *"change their minds when they see war"* (Exod. 13:17). They were put in a place where they could grow up.

Later on in the biblical account, Israel refused to enter the promise of God due to unbelief. In this case, the curse of the wilderness was punitive to some and transitional for others. Joshua and Caleb had to wait almost 40 years for all the "unbelief" to be cut out of Israel. All who had doubt died in the wilderness, without a strong voice from God. Joshua and Caleb believed and survived the same wilderness that killed all of the others. They had to wait. They were not being punished. It was a long wait, but it matured them for what God had for them in the Promised Land.

Sometimes the seeming silence of Heaven is merely a waiting period for the right timing. Ask the Joseph of the Old Testament! He was familiar with 13 years of misunderstanding and grief. He might have felt very disconnected at times, but in the end he realized the depths that the wilderness had produced in him.

Many biblical characters developed in times of solitude and inactivity. Even good people will go through times of relative silence. When the rain stops, the wells will be dug deeper. The wilderness is a time to explore that which God has placed within you.

PURPOSEFUL SILENCE

Dutch author, Henri Nouwen writes, "First silence makes us pilgrims. Secondly, silence guards the fire within. Thirdly, silence teaches us to speak."[6] Nouwen is referring to a silence on our part, but I believe there are lessons as to why God is silent at times. When God is silent, we truly become pilgrims, or explorers. The thirst for Him can consume us like the greater desire for drink when none is available. We've all experienced those first moments on a hot day when we finally quench our thirst. Similarly, silence sends us on a search, for His voice.

The absence of a voice can be unsettling for some. We're like insecure children who must speak to break the uncomfortable feeling of contemplation.

Peter felt he needed to speak on the Mount of Transfiguration. He felt that something needed to be done. The moment called for awe, yet he wanted to build something (see Matt. 17:4).

A voice came out of the cloud saying, "*Hear Him.*" (Matt. 17: 5). In other words...shhhh!

Silence will bring your search light out, drawing you into a deeper understanding of His voice. Don't be afraid! Sometimes it's good to be quiet and to hear nothing. Like Nouwen says, "You guard the fire within." The Bible says, "*Be still, and know that I am God*" (Ps. 46:10). Scripture seems to bear out that the silent times will bring a knowledge of God that no other time can.

The silence will teach us to speak. Nouwen says, "A word with power is a word that comes out of silence."[7] Again, he is referring to our need to have times of silence and places of solitude. Is it possible though that this also applies to God? After He has been silent, His next words may be marinated and saturated with time and wisdom.

Moses experienced years of solitude and silence in the wilderness after fleeing Egypt as a wanted man. He saw a burning bush that would not be consumed, and it caught his attention. Turning to look at it, a voice spoke and said, "*Moses, Moses!*"

(Exod. 3:4). This was the beginning of reentry into the destiny of God for Moses. He was hesitant, yet finally yielded to the voice that would become his lifeline in the years ahead.

Get comfortable with the fact that God not only speaks in many ways, but also in a diversity of intensity. The problem of the ages is not the lack of communication from God, but the lack of response from His people. The Book of Revelation says seven times, "*He who has an ear, let him hear...*" (Rev. 2:7, 11, 17, 29; 3:6, 13, 22).

God is talking—are we listening? Even more...are we responding?

EXPLORING THE VOICE QUESTIONS:

1. Share or remember a time when God increased His intensity of what He communicated to you. How did He do that?

2. When is silence a needed tool in communication, especially from God?

3. Why does silence teach us to speak with greater power?

DO IT YOURSELF!

The Bible refers to nine fruit of the Spirit: love, joy, peace, longsuffering, kindness, goodness, faithfulness, gentleness, and self-control. See what God sees. Look at a friend or partner and declare the fruit that is prominent in their lives. Describe the fruit and allow God to enhance its fragrance over them.

ENDNOTES

1. "Six Reasons to Improve Your Body Language," *Personal Development and People Skills* (Oct. 26, 2006), retrieved from the Internet at: http://www.positivityblog.com/index.php/2006/10/26/6-reasons-to-improve-your-body-language/.

2. Frank Bartleman, *Azusa Street* (New Kensington, PA: Whitaker House, 1982), 36.

3. Bartleman, *Azusa Street,* 34.

4. F.F. Bruce, The Book of the Acts—New International Commentary on the New Testament (Grand Rapids, MI: William B. Eerdmans, 1954).

5. Wikipedia, "Swing Low, Sweet Chariot."

6. Henri Nouwen, *The Way of the Heart* (NY: HarperCollins, 1981).

7. Nouwen, *The Way of the Heart.*

Chapter Six

THEOCACHING
WITH THE VOICE:

Looking for Heaven's Treasure in Others

But we have this treasure in earthen vessels... (2 Corinthians 4:7).

I was introduced to a new phenomenon last year while visiting Scotland. I stayed at a house where another man from America was also staying. We had the opportunity to share supper together one night. I had been training people all day, but he had been doing something quite different. He had been geocaching.

Geocaching is a modern-day form of treasure hunting. Using a GPS system, my new friend had sought out a small box hidden in the Scottish Highlands. I was intrigued and asked for more details.

As of this writing, 350,000 geocaches or treasure boxes are currently in 222 countries around the world.[1] Geocaching was birthed in 2000, as a result of a turning off of a government scrambler known as "Selective Availability." This allowed regular citizens to enjoy GPS readings with an accuracy of ten meters.

Geocaching is fairly simple. Someone hides a weatherproof box in a forest, under a bridge, or in the crook of a tree, for example. It contains a list where the explorer enters his or her name. You can also register your find on the Internet. Sometimes a small trinket is in the box, and you take it out and replace it with something else. The trinkets are of no real value except in this international sport. There are now thousands of boxes hidden all around the world, maybe even in your backyard!

My informer was excited because this "cache," or treasure, was relatively new, yet already had some 40 log entries from as far away as Japan. Some caches are more challenging than others and are rated as such on the Internet.

This particular one was well-hidden and caused them to walk back and forth through the woods following the satellite coordinates, fulfilling clues, before their final discovery. His enthusiasm was contagious!

Some participants actually put an object in a cache box with a destination that is around the globe. It's considered a "hitchhiker." Someone may place a trinket in a park in Texas with a destination for Australia. Participants help by taking the trinket and traveling with it to another cache until it eventually arrives at its destination. All of this can be tracked on the Internet. My new friend already visited numerous sites around the world and was keeping track of it on his Internet site.

CHRISTMAS FIND

The following Christmas, a family member gave me my Christmas present in the form of GPS coordinates. Using my new handheld GPS system, I headed off in search of my other presents. There I was on Christmas day, trudging through the snow, in search of my very own present. This was my introduction to geocaching.

Geocaching combines the innate desire to explore with the overwhelming joys of discovery. The excitement raced through my veins as the kid in me came out. I found a little plastic box with a DVD tucked safely inside of it, strategically placed in shrubs near a dam. What fun! It also had coordinates for my next gift, and off I went on another treasure hunt on Christmas Day.

There comes a time in every rightly constructed boy's life when he has a raging desire to go somewhere and dig for hidden treasure.

—Henry A. Kissinger (1923-)

It dawned on me that people were treasures also. Locked up secretly in every person is a destiny (cache) designed by God Himself. Is it possible that we have been called to hunt treasures in one another? Finding just the right combination takes time. Decades of marriage have taught me that not only is a woman a treasure that needs to be discovered, but the combination keeps changing! Our greatest times together as a couple are those moments of discovery. A moment is unveiled that reveals an understanding about how your partner thinks and what's really important in their life. Now that's a treasure worth searching for!

Jesus said that where our treasure is, our heart would be there also (see Matt. 6:21). Finding the destiny treasure in someone will connect you to their heart in a way nothing else will. You must have the ability to hear the voice of Heaven and then use that knowledge to search out a deep thing in someone else. God will help you find the deep wealth of another if you will volunteer for the adventure.

Close Encounters

It reminds me of the movie, *Close Encounters of the Third Kind*. In that movie, a variety of people were touched with special knowledge that made them passionate, almost crazy. The star of the movie is compelled to gather dirt in his living room and begin to shape a mountain. Of course, everyone thinks he is insane. Extreme passion can appear as insanity, due to its compelling focus. It turns out that he was getting a partial picture of an alien encounter that was about to take place. It also turns out that many other people were given the same revelation and wound up being drawn to the same place...for an encounter of the third kind! In that moment, it all began to make sense. They were no longer the "crazies" who heard strange voices, but an elect few who would experience something unique and powerful.

Passion to Search

Heaven wants to grip us with a passion to search, even though we may not have all the details. The same way that a signal comes from the heavens to show us the coordinates on a GPS, so can a signal from above show you where you are and where you are going. It can also help you assist friends in discovering their Heaven-sent destiny.

Once a clear signal begins to come from Heaven, move on from just hoarding it for yourself and use it to benefit all who are groping in the darkness. Become like someone who has discovered a torch in a dark cave. How can you leave others in the dark?

You would be amazed at the hidden treasures that lie all around us. Sometimes it takes sifting through mounds of history or hurt. Treasures are usually protected well. The greater the value of a cache, the more illusive it may be. You might actually stumble upon the wealth of a person's heart by accident. A window of revelation may open in a moment when they have become vulnerable. Treasures, especially human treasures, must be treated with respect and awe.

Valuable Surprises

My mother passed away several years ago and my brother, sister, and I were going through her years of accumulated stuff. Most of what was in boxes was insignificant letters or financial records. We were being fairly aggressive in throwing things away when all of a sudden, my sister, Pam, said, "This might have value." She was referring to a fancy program of a banquet in California that my mother and father had attended 30 years prior. It was interesting.

Apparently the banquet had a five-star listing of guests, including famous comedienne Lucille Ball, singer Frank Sinatra, KFC founder Colonel Sanders, comedian Bob Hope, and others. My father had apparently walked around the banquet and gathered autographs on the program...over one dozen famous signatures!

The atmosphere changed as the worth of the program was instantly upgraded from trash to an article worthy of careful handling and close scrutiny. It was only a paper among many, but now it had graduated to a treasure. How close we came to tossing it out with the other junk! You never know what might be hidden in a pile of paper.

A box without hinges, key, or lid, yet golden treasure inside is hid.

—J. R. R. Tolkien (1892-1973)

Actually, you may never know what is hidden in the person sitting next to you at school or work. There might be a sunken ship with a hull full of gold in that heart beating near yours. Only a treasure hunter can uncover it. A well-seasoned hearer of God's voice will see and discover the otherwise overlooked value of life.

Sometimes treasures are hidden in ornate boxes or great tombs. The Bible says that the treasure that God places within humans is in a simple vessel…earthen. In other words, it appears to be of little value. A treasure might be contained within someone of low education, or a child, or someone restricted to a nursing facility. The explorer might be fooled to look for true treasure elsewhere.

In 1989, a Philadelphia man innocently found a treasure in an old painting that he had purchased for $4 at a flea market. He had bought the painting of a country scene because he liked the frame. In his attempt to detach the frame from the picture, it fell apart in his hands. When that happened, he found a folded document that had been placed between the painting and the backing—and it appeared to be a copy of the Declaration of Independence! It turned out to be one of the original 500 official copies of that sacred document. Only 24 similar copies were known to be in existence. The remarkably intact document fetched a healthy $2.42 million at an auction. Not a bad return for a $4 investment![2]

ANCIENT TREASURE HUNTERS

The wise men in the Bible were the original "Theocachers," or God searchers. They followed a sign from Heaven, a star, to the very side of Jesus Himself. I've seen the same bumper sticker that you've probably seen, which says: "Wise Men Still Seek Him."

The voice from Heaven is still speaking, calling us to seek out and discover the hidden treasures all around. I have been a part of "prophetic" groups that listen to Heaven and then act on what we have received. This can be done in a normal conversation, or in a targeted way toward those in need. I remember where one such team ventured out together. They had each sought to hear from Heaven and had received bits and pieces of understanding. They went out and bought a bag of groceries and followed the heavenly GPS in their hearts. They turned down the street that one had seen and finally saw the house that fit the indication of their heart.

Knocking on the door, they found a family that was in need. Not only did they give the groceries that they had purchased to fulfill their need, but they also spent time praying and comforting the family. Does Heaven participate in our lives in this manner? Apparently so!

How will you know that you are truly hearing from God? How can you judge one another's impressions with any sense of accuracy? It helps to be a part of a training group with accountability. Is what I'm hearing truly coming from Heaven? Here are some basic guidelines for treasure hunting in the lives of others.

Treasure Hunting Rules

1. **My stuff or Heaven's?** Never share an insight about something that you already have strong opinions on. The less connected you are personally with someone, the more likely that what you share will be pure and unpolluted by opinion. Your own emotions about a situation will cloud what Heaven is really wanting to say. Leave these insights for others. If you truly discern something for someone you know,

turn it into private prayer. Prayer instead of share is always a good guideline.

2. **Contradicting the truth of eternity?** What we communicate and sense must line up with the text of the Bible. Is what I'm hearing actually opposing what God would say in a situation? Only a solid knowledge of God's ways will protect you from error.

3. **Is my communication redemptive?** Does it produce hope and a way out? Heaven loves us so much that God always provides an escape. Everything that we share must be laced with a redemptive purpose. If you don't know what it is, then don't share it with someone else!

4. **Will I strengthen or weaken?** Heaven's voice places a high value on encouragement and building. Everything we share has to be with the intent of facilitating growth and construction. We always want to leave people better off than before we spoke to them. The attitude in which we share insights needs to have a language of hope. Kind, gentle words will add to every communication we share.

POLLUTED WATERS

Gossip is destructive. I believe it is the opposite of the voice from Heaven. Its origins are evil and destructive. If you speak in patterns of backbiting and gossip, it will program you in such a way that perverts your ability to encourage. Whatever you are programming into your communication will come out in all of your endeavors.

You will always be thwarted in building a life of encouragement if you have a lifestyle of gossip. Like a cancer, it will eat at the bread of life, leaving nothing of spiritual or emotional value. When you try to encourage someone with an insight from Heaven, it will have the taste of you instead of Heaven.

Live in such a way that you would not be ashamed to sell your parrot to the town gossip.

—Will Rogers (1879-1935)

In a fashion similar to John the Baptist, we endeavor to have more of Heaven and less of us. The phrase, "*He must increase, but I must decrease*" (John 3:30), sums up the proper platform for a launching of effective communication of Heaven's voice.

Have you ever drunk from a garden hose on a hot summer day? What does it taste like? I know...it tastes hosey! It tastes more like the hose than the refreshing water that flows in the high places.

On the other hand, drinking from a fresh mountain spring tastes like Heaven! People whom we are encouraging need to taste more of Heaven and less of us. We are the conduit for Heaven's voice, and we need to be clean. Commit to changing your patterns. If necessary, remove yourself from relationships that promote hellish gossip and plant yourself among the encouragers. Program your spirit to feed on good food.

I went through a one-month physical detox program to improve my health. It was shortly after my 50th birthday and felt like a 100,000-mile checkup. I went through daily cleansing and restructuring of my eating habits. I was restricted to eating certain vegetables only for one month.

The only fluid I could drink was water and also an occasional smoothie. At first it was grueling. All I could think of was pizza and sweets. As the days went by, my body began to change and crave healthy foods.

One of my daughters made brownies and the smell filled the house. I was surprised that I wasn't tempted to rob the pan. I had reprogrammed my system to seek health. Don't get me wrong— I can still be tempted and even succumb, but my life leans toward health. You can produce the environment that will allow for a non-polluted flow from Heaven to you and to others!

The following chart may help in judging whether something has originated in Heaven or in someone's mind. Many will think that they are speaking on behalf of God when talking to you. How do you know what is really the voice of Heaven? Is there a way to judge and how do we respond to others who speak into our lives? Check this out:

EXPLANATION OF THE CHART

I. *Simple* **Prophecy** — This is the sharing of simple words from Heaven that would encourage or comfort.

Chart D

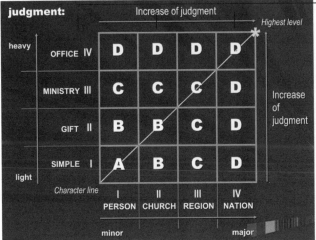

Obviously, judgment on this level would be very low. This is the average person who would communicate to each of us an impression.

II. *Gift* of Prophecy — This involves a person who has an extraordinary ability to perceive situations and people. They are able to know the voice of Heaven in an almost supernatural way. Due to that gifting, a greater judgment, or expectation, would be upon them to be loving and accurate.

III. Prophetic *Ministry* — This is a person who gives a significant portion of their life to ministering and serving through special insight. They might teach, equip, or declare words that are weightier and broader, impacting larger groups of people. Their position demands a stricter accountability because of the platform they have.

IV. *Office* **of the Prophet** — This is a person who has been gifted by God with insights that are profound, accompanied by signs and potentially miracles. Typically, their very lives are a "message" from Heaven. They are sought out for particular solutions and wisdom. They usually speak with a potency that comes with a high office. They would get the closest scrutiny because their office affords them great opportunity for abuse.

The levels that go from left to right on the chart speak of the size of the audience to whom a word from Heaven is being communicated. In other words, we not only judge the person communicating the word, but also the sphere of audience. A simple prophecy would have low judgment unless it was given to a large group. The impact of how many it touches raises the intensity of potential blessing or damage.

The lettering on the chart is interpreted as follows:

A. **The A Zone** — No judgment necessary for "simple prophecy," just keep it light and coach for greater accuracy and detail.

B. **The B Zone** — Follow guidelines of the place you are ministering into. Submit to those who are in authority where you are speaking, be it a business, family, church, or government. Learn to judge the person even more than the word. Are they a vessel without an agenda? Watch for a developing track record of loving communication with beneficial results.

C. **The C Zone** — Encourage growth. Seek references from someone communicating at this level. Where do they come from, and are they celebrated where they live? Deal strongly with error. They are at a level, or communicating a level, that can be dangerous if they are functioning in a wrong spirit. If errors occur, establish probationary seasons for restoration of the person back into functional service.

D. **The D Zone** — Hold this person or situation to the highest level of accountability. Judge it severely with a restorative heart. Hold the "Prophet" to the fulfillment of the word. If a word is about the future, then it needs to be judged accordingly. If severe error is made, then appeal to the one delivering the word or their accountability. Words that rise to the level of directing a nation or large group of people should be taken seriously and agreement made or judgment rendered.

As we seek the treasure in one another we will begin to build a reputation for having heavenly solutions. Always keep a teachable heart, and God may exalt your words to direct a nation in a time of need.

Martin Luther King Jr. found such words, as did Abraham Lincoln and many others. Who knows what treasure might lie deep in your heart? Let others mine it out of you, and search your own heart, readily giving words of encouragement to others around you. Through this your sphere of influence will increase. Your ability to hear will increase also. Soon, you'll be a treasure hunter seeking out the lost treasures all around you. What is Heaven's voice saying about that person next to you?

EXPLORING THE VOICE QUESTIONS:

1. What is the treasure that you can find in at least three other people?

2. What hides the treasure in most people?

3. How might we find treasures in people we have known for many years?

4. How does it benefit our relationships to continue searching for deeper riches in one another?

DO IT YOURSELF!

Get in a group and target an individual to explore. Look for hidden treasures as Heaven reveals the gem in each participant.

Gather a group of treasure hunters and seek Heaven's insight together. Write down the information received and launch out into the marketplace searching for a recipient. Share your insights to the agreed upon recipient.

ENDNOTES

1. Wikipedia, "Geocaching."

2. Information retrieved on the Internet at:
    http://www.snopes.com/luck/declare.asp.

Chapter Seven

WHAT DO I DO
WITH THE VOICE?

*Putting Heaven's Words
Into Practical Action*

*For the vision is yet for an appointed time; but at the end
it will speak, and it will not lie. Though it tarries, wait for
it; because it will surely come, it will not tarry* (Habakkuk
2:3).

I knew that my time in Canada was about over. I had experienced ten great years of teaching, training, and personal development. I had been working in establishing churches and training for an international business course. Something deep inside of me was alerting me that a change was coming. Have you ever felt that? It's almost intangible, yet it brings an atmospheric change that is undeniable. This time it wasn't circumstantial. Everything was going well; in fact, after eight challenging years, I finally had several momentum years that were producing great fruit. I was happy and willing to spend the rest of my life in that location.

Several indicators were catching my attention though. You know…the odd circumstances that inform you that transition is imminent. As I mentioned in Chapter One, I was on a flight to Florida, and while sitting back, settling in for a two-hour flight, I noticed the in-flight Continental Airline magazine. Grabbing it from the seat pocket, I scanned the cover, which referred to Cleveland, Ohio, the place of my birth. I can't explain what happened, but something churned inside that caught my curiosity. It turned out to be a major hint of what was about to unfold in my life. Small things can add up to something big, when your spiritual eyes and ears are tuned in.

In a moment of decision the best thing you can do is the right thing. The worst thing you can do is nothing.

—*Theodore Roosevelt (1858-1919)*

"TURNING POINT" WORDS

One month later I was on a plane to Japan, and out of the blue, a friend turned to me and said that I was about to be invited back to Cleveland. (I mention this again to illustrate the process that was happening in my mind.) Cleveland would not have been my first choice. In fact, I had told my wife that if we ever moved from Canada, we should consider a southern city, where it was warm.

Cleveland did not seem to line up with what I was really feeling inside, but the two encounters happening back to back made me wonder. I've come to know these as familiar fingerprints of Heaven.

Returning home from my Japan trip, I found an invitation lying on my desk to speak in Cleveland. What a surprise! I began to get suspicious. I had not had an invitation to speak in that city since I left—ten years previous. This definitely had the fingerprint of Heaven on it. Yet, this would be a major move, so I needed greater confirmation. I would never make a major decision based on an impression or a couple of circumstances.

Step by step, I moved through the process, attempting to discern and learn what Heaven was saying to me. I have to admit, I had several sleepless nights as I pondered this major decision. Was I supposed to move? Major decisions impact everything in your life. This decision would impact me, my family, my finances, and my future. A wrong move would not be easily corrected.

Several months later, I moved and have been living in Cleveland ever since. It was the right move. It was the proper timing. I used a simple technique that has helped me with discerning Heaven's voice over my own feelings.

How can we know that the timing is right and that we are really hearing truth from Heaven and not just the voice of well-meaning friends and counselors?

Feeling the Direction?

When it comes to major decisions, we need more than just a feeling. We appreciate input from others, but many times it becomes a chorus of voices that speak different languages, diverse destinies. Those who are close to us can become clouded by their dreams for us, not wanting us to move away or progress in a pattern that has not been their expectation for us. Having said that, I do believe that wisdom can be found in the counsel of many (see Proverbs 24:6). Wisdom is not the counsel of many, but it can be found in it.

Our lives are a sum total of the choices we have made.

—Wayne Dyer (1940-)

Careful consideration is needed in making choices. Points of view need to be heard, but the most important is the still, small voice that whispers in your heart in a place of solitude. It originates in Heaven and has a perspective that can rightly align all of your days. Is there a way to systematically unravel the mysteries of everyday life? Who will I marry? Where will I live? Should I take this job or wait for another? What kind of training would be appropriate in pursuit of a career?

Not a Science

First of all, it goes without saying that this is not a science. It truly is an art form…learning to discern. You will make mistakes. Your batting average will improve though, as you practice on less impacting decisions in life.

My son Josh was talking to his sister on the phone who was planning a mission trip. She had been living in California attending a school and needed a large sum of money for the journey. She jokingly said to Josh, "Hey, are you going to support me in my mission trip?"

Josh chuckled and was about to decline, when he glanced across our street and saw an unusual sight. The lights on the lawn of our neighbor's house were cascading up the evergreen trees forming an odd shaping of letters. The wind was blowing, but the sign was clear. The shape of the trees forged the light into the formation of the word: "Give."

He was stunned and called me in to witness it. Sure enough, even with the wind blowing, those letters spelled out a message from Heaven!

Josh contributed a sizable sum of money for his young years, and he reaped a great reward in return. Heaven loves to work in our lives in naturally supernatural ways. The signs are all around us.

When you build up a history of hearing Heaven's voice, you also begin to build confidence. What a difference it makes when you can look a major challenge in the eye and move with peace and confidence! Let's look closely at the following chart that I developed to assist in practically understanding the revelation or information that you are receiving and how to respond to it.

RISK AND RESPONSE

The chart is broken up into four sections that represent places that we find ourselves in during the decision-making process. Where you are in the chart depends on several components. The vertical line up the left side, entitled "Risk," represents whether the action you want to take is considered high or low risk. If it involves one of life's major decisions then it would be high risk. Those major initiatives may include marriage, relocation, career, friendships, education, etc. These topics will locate you in one of the top two boxes, number three or two. If it helps you in this process, you may want to color box number one *green* for go, number two *yellow* for caution, and number three *red* for stop.

The two upper boxes represent high-risk moves, and the lower two boxes are for low-risk decisions. If you are ready to purchase a car, you can test this box. Ask yourself, "Is this a high-risk venture?" Depending on your personal income and the type of car you're buying, you might say, "Yes." This would put it into box number two or three.

You might note the lower horizontal line entitled "Response." This line measures your personal response to the decision. Do you have high energy, faith, and confidence that this can happen? If so, then you would fit into one of the right boxes, either number one or two. Study the chart for a moment…

If you were about to purchase a car that was a high risk and you are doubtful as to whether it will work out for you, then you are in box number three. Do not make major decisions if you are in box number three. I have waited up to two years before making a purchase if it falls into box number three.

CHART E: REVELATION RESPONSE CHART

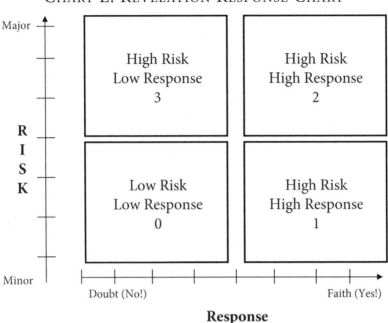

If your purchase is a low risk and you have the cash to pay for it, then it may fall into box number one. Anything that falls into box number one is a green light. You can move ahead with confidence!

Let's try another possible circumstance. Let's say that you are offered a job several thousand miles away. You're getting advice, but it's all over the place. Friends are telling you to go for it, yet family members are begging you to stay. You believe that Heaven has given you the OK, but you still have hesitations. You first need to determine if this is a high-risk move. The level of risk involved may depend on whether you are married, have children, or will be leaving strong family support systems.

Let's say that you determine it is high risk, but your response is one of excitement and faith. You really do believe that Heaven has opened this door. What do you do? Let's look at the four quadrants of the chart and what your action should be if you find yourself located in one of them.

0 = Low Risk/Low Response

God is in the business of stretching us. For that reason, I question if these things—situations that fall in the low risk/low response category—are even God speaking. If someone or some circumstance indicates to you an action that occurs in box zero, ignore it unless it's confirmed. Your faith and vision may need to grow. Heaven's voice is calling you into a greater place of faith and risk. Put a demand on yourself to be creative and adventurous. Put yourself into places where you will need to hear from Heaven or you will fail!

1 = Low Risk/High Response

This is the best place to be. It's the green light. You can move in faith and safety. The risk is low—not because the situation is unimportant or trivial, but because your faith has grown and your trust in what Heaven has told you has increased. Your high-faith response will blast you through any minor barriers that you may encounter.

Let's say that you are contemplating a major career choice. Maybe the pay for the new job is similar to what you earn now, but opportunities abound in the new position. The risk is relatively low, but maybe doubts are clouding your mind. Obviously, your faith response, that "yes" deep inside of you, needs to increase. Information will not increase your faith. Your response needs to increase due to a feeding of that eternal part of you that will ultimately rule over every doubt—your spirit.

Your spirit feeds on and grows through food from Heaven. The Bible is your buffet. Daily doses of meditation on the Bible will increase your faith and shrink your doubt. You need to increase your faith response, so get reading, meditating, and if necessary memorize key Bible verses that pertain to your situation. May I suggest a few for this situation:

The steps of a good man are ordered by the Lord, and He delights in his way. Though he fall, he shall not be utterly cast down; for the Lord upholds him with His hand (Psalm 37:23-24).

Meditation and gentle repeating of this verse will firmly plant you into box number one. Once you realize that you have been established in a place of confidence, you can proceed regardless of what obstacles may present themselves.

This verse might be another one that you would consider:

The plans of the diligent lead surely to plenty, but those of everyone who is hasty, surely to poverty (Proverbs 21:5).

Hasty decisions will lead to great pain. You are a planner though. You will only move ahead as you gain a confidence that goes beyond understanding. Heaven is on your side, and you will not fail!

This confidence has been developed in a back room consulting with Heaven. You can make decisions with an assurance when you sense that Heaven is partnering with you!

A Confident Edge

Your secret to decision making gives you an edge. You will stand out among other employees as a decision maker. You are filling your heart with a power that doesn't come from a self-help book. Self-help uses *your* strength; that's why it's called "self" help. No doubt, it has power, but the kind of authority you need will only be developed with Heaven's assistance. We must become familiar with Heaven's voice.

Another way to increase your assurance that the timing is right to move ahead is by prayer. I'm not talking about religious prayers that you have heard or prayed yourself. Many of those prayers originate in your mind. They have a hope attached, but it is more akin to the kind of confidence that is associated with scratching a lotto ticket. You might "hit it" and you might not. Many of us might throw some prayers up, but our actions speak that we have little confidence in Heaven's power.

The "Knower"

Major decisions demand a different type of prayer. This kind of prayer will not only bring results from Heaven, but will also build up your eternal spirit. It comes from the gut. Many have called it the "knower"—that place in you that isn't just a misty eye at a funeral, but brings gut-wrenching mourning at the loss of a friend. It's that inner being that brings outrageous laughter at times that are not convenient. It's beyond normal and leaves you with a sense that you have experienced something that is other-worldly, eternal, even spiritually supernatural. It's called the "knower" because all at once you just know that you *are* communicating with Heaven.

The only real valuable thing is intuition.

—*Albert Einstein (1879-1955)*

This type of prayer—prayer that springs forth from your innermost parts—can come at times of desperation or in the simple moments of waiting quietly on God. I was hit with this several weeks ago. I was praying about someone else and their deep sorrow. Suddenly, I was overwhelmed with a groaning that pushed my prayers into a different place. In that moment, I felt what the other person felt. I became a true intercessor in a time when I didn't know what to do. In that place, Heaven partners with you and prays in a way that brings results and truly changes you in the process.

The Bible hints about these moments as you can read in this passage:

Likewise the Spirit also helps in our weaknesses. For we do not know what we should pray for as we ought, but the Spirit Himself makes intercession for us with groanings which cannot be uttered. Now He who searches the hearts knows what the mind of the Spirit is, because He makes intercession for the saints according to the will of God (Romans 8:26-27).

Simply stated…the Holy Spirit prays through us. Later in the Bible it states that this type of prayer literally builds us up.

But you, beloved, building yourselves up on your most holy faith, praying in the Holy Spirit (Jude 1:20).

As you are "built up," you move ahead. This doesn't mean that there will not be challenges, but your Heaven-sent strength will easily conquer them. Your life has placed you in box number one: a place of high faith and excitement with low risk. *Count your blessings!*

If an obstacle arises, joyfully move it. Do not allow yourself to be stopped. This should be a goal of our life to live in this place or at least close to it. This is the garden of Eden, a place of communing with God without fear. A guiding hand will bring you through to victory. Now…what do you do if you are stuck in box two or three?

2 = High Risk/High Response

I was faced with an opportunity last year. I had been hoping for such, but it's a different story when it knocks on your door. My son had voiced several times that when he graduates from high school he would like to design, build, and renovate homes. I had been praying for a small project for us to do together. After all, "hands-on" learning is the best way to find out how to prosper at something. The problem was, I had never done anything quite like this before.

A friend of mine was developing a large tract of land for building. He had purchased two homes on the road to make way for the development. He tore down one home and took a small section of the backyard of the other. This little house was a perfect practice house for my son and me. My friend offered it to me, and I was faced with a box-two scenario. I was excited about it, but due to my lack of experience was also intimidated by it.

I took several days to decide fully, during which time I sat myself in a bookstore reading every book I could find on the subject. Information began to decrease the risk in my mind. I was lowering myself from a box two to a box one. My faith was high, but obstructed by the obvious lack-of-knowledge barriers. I needed to lower the risk level in my own mind. Through my research, it dropped, and I bought the house. What a time we had doing some demolition, working with contractors, making decisions, installing cabinets, and eventually selling it for profit. My son got a trip to Scotland as a reward, and I got a motorcycle! It was well worth the risk, and my son's confidence has increased due to the experience. (Of course, now I've created a monster. He now wants to tackle something again…but even bigger!)

Putting Risk in a Proper Place

In box two, it's all about decreasing the risk in your own mind. A popular biblical character who faced a situation that would fit in this box would be Noah. He heard from Heaven that he was supposed to build a large boat in the middle of the desert! That's high risk! Amazingly enough, Noah seemed to not question this task. He was up for it. He had confidence in both the person giving him the task—God—and in his own ability to understand and act upon God's instructions.

The Bible says that Noah "*walked with God*" (Gen. 6:9). To his credit, he did this in one of the most perverse environments in human history. The opposition to what Noah was doing must have been fierce, yet goes unmentioned in the Bible. Noah must have known Heaven's ways and therefore was in great faith for what God required of him. The Bible says that he "*moved with godly fear*" (Heb. 11:7). He had a respect for God, and it showed in his obedience to Heaven's voice.

Only those who will risk going too far can possibly find out how far one can go.

—T.S. Eliot (1888-1965)

The interesting part of this story that probably slipped it from a box two to a box one was the details that God gave him. God made it easier for Noah by telling him the size of the boat, what to make it with, and when to get in it. That kind of detailed instruction would decrease the risk factor and energize Noah to move ahead as if he was in a box-one situation.

Water-Walking Risk

Peter, the disciple of Jesus, was invited by Him to walk on water. I believe this would fall into the "high risk" zone of decisions. Peter doesn't hesitate, but jumps out of the boat and does the impossible. His faith started out high but was immediately impacted by the circumstances around him. He began to sink, having spied the wind and the waves.

Now, I can't criticize Peter. After all, what he did was extraordinary. I have never walked on water! Yet, what we learn from Peter's example is that it would benefit us to keep our lives and eyes focused on what God said, and He will help us avoid devastating endings.

How do you move from a box two, which is a "caution yellow," to a box one, which is green for "go"? You do so by understanding what is being asked of you and proceeding slowly. In fact, anything that falls into the top half of the chart should bring us to a slower process. If you find yourself in a decision that fits into high risk/high faith response, you may want to follow this path: Get the facts and seek spiritual counsel and confirmation.

Get the Facts!

Gain information to lower the risk in your mind. It is also important to pause in order to allow a greater view to appear. The general rule of engagement is this: "If you need an answer now, then the answer is no!" One of the best lessons to learn in decision making is the ability to firmly say, "No!" You can't always avoid having a narrow perspective, but you must attempt to arm yourself with as much information as possible as you proceed with caution.

Thinking about marriage? If you move on a sense of "faith response" alone, you may end up devastated. What about money decisions? Emotional buys on the stock market can destroy your finances. The sense of "confirmation" that we all feel during emotional decisions can't always be trusted. Yet it's difficult to separate what is from Heaven and what is from your own mind when it is fogged by emotion.

Moving with your "gut" may sound spiritual or daring, but can quickly erode years of labor. Take decisions slowly. Create a history of good, informed decision making. In time, you will be able to move quicker because wisdom will start developing, and your confidence will grow. Your senses will be trained to spot an opportunity, access it with due diligence, and strike with growing success.

Spiritual Counsel and Confirmation

Spiritual counsel and mentoring can be helpful as you grow. Young adults especially need to find a successful person who is doing what they want to do and attach themselves to them! There are three basic paths to maturity: You can learn from your own mistakes, learn from the mistakes of others, or study and apply what the Bible teaches. I think you know the best choices!

When you are faced with a life choice, before you firmly make a decision, look for confirmations. Does it appear that everything is lining up in your favor? Does it seem like you are looking through a pair of binoculars and everything is coming into focus? Work the problem slowly, waiting for the signs that appear and show you the way. Heaven is on your side!

Confirmation will come. Don't be in a hurry, especially about major decisions. Life will hold many opportunities, and you will learn when to move faster. Right now...work on your timing! You may need more clues for the action to be consummated.

There is as much difference between the counsel that a friend giveth, and that a man giveth himself, as there is between the counsel of a friend and of a flatterer. For there is no such flatterer as is a man's self.

—*Francis Bacon (1561-1626)*

---

3 = High Risk/Low Response

This is *not* the place you want to stay! We all will visit this spot in life many times. Your ultimate goal is to learn how to navigate the waters of fear into a place of peace. This is the "red zone." No decisions should be made in this place. Did you get that? *No decisions should be made in this box.* Your hope is to slowly, intelligently move to a safer place.

In this box number three is the challenge that is high risk, yet you have little or no faith to move ahead. In fact, you may be plagued with doubt or fear. Short-term fear can be your friend. A healthy fear makes me put on my motorcycle helmet even though it's not required by law. Healthy fear keeps me out of the large waves at the ocean because I do not swim well! This "healthy" fear could also be called caution or even wisdom. Wisdom keeps me eating healthy because I've seen and experienced the penalty of haphazard living.

Sometimes fears and doubts may be the signal that you are not ready for a major decision. I'm not saying that God produces the fear. Fear is present in the absence of true faith. Light is the only thing that drives darkness (fear) away. Someone needs to turn the lights on. Revelation and illumination is essential.

If you are facing a large business deal, yet have a nagging "hold" in your stomach…listen to it! It doesn't mean that you will miss the deal, although that may end up not being a bad thing! It just means that the environment and landscape need to change for you to move ahead in boldness. If it seems "too good to be true," then it probably is, and you should let it go by. The "once in a lifetime" deal will come more often than you think.

I could tell many stories where people I know have overridden the hesitation in their spirit only to regret it later. Men and women have proceeded with their weddings even though they had major concerns and struggles, beyond the normal queasiness of matrimony. Others have made major financial decisions on a whim because of "once in a lifetime" opportunities that appeared. One friend of mine felt the pressure from others during the tech boom of the late 1990s. He took his retirement money out of relatively safe mutual funds and bought individual stocks, losing almost everything. These snap decisions usually end in disaster.

Time-Share Blues

I remember one time, shortly after I was married, my wife and I were presented with a time-share opportunity. It was one of those opportunities where you attend a one-hour presentation in exchange for a coupon for free dinner at an expensive place. It seemed like an easy exchange, my time for their money. We did the tour of the beautiful property; then came the hard sell. I had no interest, nor did I have the money, yet they pitched on! Phones were ringing all around us as salesmen celebrated more sales. A bell was rung anytime a time-share was sold. Bells were ringing every few minutes. The pressure was building. My salesman informed me that time was running out, and soon all of the units would be accounted for.

He pitched it from every angle. "This is a great investment! Your future children will use it. You can exchange it for anywhere in the world. You deserve it! Quit renting and own!" Finally in visible melodramatic frustration, he said, "What would hinder you from this great deal?" Having no money could not be the answer. He had already offered a low interest, complete financing deal that was "today only." I sat quietly and then cleverly proclaimed that I make no major decisions without consulting with my Father. He said, "Call him," and slammed a phone down on the desk. I was trapped. Finally, with a feeling of great intimidation and some shame I said, "Look…I just came in here for the free dinner, can I have the coupon?" Yeah, Steve! He reached in the desk in a disgusted fashion, handed me the gift certificate, and left me with the feeling of having lost a close friend. My wife and I were frazzled, and we never went back to one of those presentations again. I know that those salespeople sold scores of those units each day though.

Many people are intimidated into making major decisions by the power of emotion or relationship. However, resolve must rule the day when it comes to right choices. Stand firm! Make the choice when the timing is right. You'll seldom regret it!

Moving out of box three has challenges. There must be an increase of your faith, and meditation and prayer will be keys.

When you see how the President makes political or policy decisions, you see who he is. The essence of the Presidency is decision making.

—*Bob Woodward (1943-)*

PRACTICAL ADVICE FOR MAKING TOUGH DECISIONS

Here is some advice to the pilgrims of decision making:

1. **Take no action** if you find yourself in box number three. You are supposed to wait. Put your dream on the shelf of silence until strong indicators permit you to advance again. Maybe you should forget about it. If it's truly from Heaven…it will reappear.

2. **Clear your mind and spirit.** One of the best ways to do this is by fasting. This may involve food but could involve entertainment as well. Fasting is a self-imposed restraint from participation in an activity. Consider a day away to retreat by yourself or with your spouse. Find a location that refreshes your soul. Fasting silences the voices of your flesh and enhances the voice from Heaven.

3. **Receive spiritual counsel and look for strong confirmations.** Once again, find that mentor or spiritual mom or dad to advise you. Weigh their viewpoint in light of what you have heard from Heaven. Listen closely to their cautions in this particular circumstance.

4. **Consider a fleece.** Yea...that's right...like the lamb's wool! The biblical character named Gideon needed strong reinforcement before he could do what he thought Heaven was requiring (Judg. 6:36-38). He laid out a fleece on the ground and asked God to make it wet but allow the ground around it to remain dry. This was the beginning of a series of tests that he put to God for confirmation. Normally, I disagree with this, but in major situations where you need strong confirmation, I believe it's acceptable. Be careful though. It can become a cheap substitute for developing a keen ear to hear from God. It can be addictive, so use this method sparingly. Faith must live in the realm of the unseen or it ceases to be faith anymore. Force yourself to learn the art of hearing and responding to the unseen. Remember this verse in the Bible:

For we walk by faith, not by sight (2 Corinthians 5:7).

A fleece can be any scenario that requests that God make Himself known in an unusual way. It typically involves God confirming something in a way that is impossible or almost impossible. It may involve an outstanding sign that would be difficult to explain in any other way than God.

For example, if you are seeking a job, you might hold all the applications before God in prayer and say, "I need $30,000 a year. I will go with the job that offers this." You might ask God to have an employer call you and make an offer where you haven't even applied. Don't be afraid to challenge God...just don't make it a habit!

Nothing can substitute direct input from Heaven. Our God in Heaven speaks in audible voices, through angels, and in signs in the heavens and Earth. Most of life's big decisions are left to our ability to read and understand Heaven's subtle indicators. Become an expert at hearing Him, and success will naturally follow.

Exploring the Voice Questions:

1. What would you classify as a major decision?

2. What people are in your life who have the power to shut down your decision with their counsel?

3. What is a major decision that you are facing now and what is going to be your approach?

Do It Yourself!

Meet in a group and help one another solve major decision challenges.

Put the template of the chart over past decisions you have made. How did you do? Assess and evaluate your decision-making "batting average."

Chapter Eight

WAITING FOR FULFILLMENT:

Gestation Period of Heaven's Voice

Until the time that his word came to pass, the word of the Lord tested him (Psalm 105:19).

HURRY TO WAIT

A H…that period of waiting. Waiting seems to be significant to Heaven. Waiting, although despised by humans, is celebrated in Heaven. Jesus left His disciples with the impression that He would soon return. Here we are 2,000 years later, and He has not yet reappeared. His definition of "soon" is obviously different from ours. His patience is something that we are unfamiliar with. There must be a greater benefit to His ultimate plan and for our eternal development in the art of waiting.

The above verse from the Bible is a puzzling, yet revealing one. The verse is a summation of the story of Joseph, who was betrayed by his brothers, sold into slavery, and who faced multiple misunderstandings and painful situations. This verse suggests that the word that Joseph had received from Heaven was in fact the restrainer of his life. Is it possible that the very destiny words that are spoken over our lives from Heaven are the shapers of who we are? Do they sculpt us like a master craftsman? Do words have that level of power? Apparently, they do!

The verse also suggests that the word was the instrument by which Heaven tested him. This could make a person less eager to hear from Heaven! The words from Heaven act like agitators in a washing machine...working out every spot and blemish that might hinder the ultimate brightness of your life.

Patience is the companion of wisdom.

—*Saint Augustine (354-430)*

In the Old Testament story, we see that when Joseph was young, he was given a powerful dream regarding his future destiny. According to the dream, those who were around him would ultimately be under his authority. However, the sharing of the revelation became the beginning of Joseph's troubles. We can learn a great lesson from this story: Be careful "who and when" you share words from Heaven with. Jealousy and envy are common and deadly.

Some lifetime words are meant to stay hidden for a season. When you hear something from Heaven, the natural tendency is to share what has been unveiled. You want to share the powerful experience and receive feedback from others. It's possible that the greatest of revelations over your life will take a lifetime to manifest. Tread softly when communicating.

I once shared a dream that I had with some friends, and it ended up costing me my job and my friendships. Not everyone is as quick to celebrate your newfound enthusiasm!

KANSAS CITY OPENER

In 1990, I was attending a conference in Kansas City. Through a series of connections that were arranged by Heaven itself, I ended up in a room with a number of people renown for hearing God's voice. I was sitting at a lunch table with a group of relative strangers only known to me as the authors and teachers of "hearing God's voice." It was awkward, yet exciting. I had hoped to meet and have an opportunity to rub shoulders with such individuals. I sat quietly and listened, like a bat boy at a major-league game. I was blessed to just be in their conversations.

One of the men whom I professionally admired, kept glancing over at me with that "Who are you and why are you here" look. Finally, he directed his conversation my way. He said, "Who are you?"

I gave him the 60-second rundown of why I was in the room and who had invited me. He then spoke to me with piercing eyes that haunted my soul. Like a treasure hunter probing deeper in the sunken ship, he said, "Are you a writer?"

I quickly replied, "No."

The conversation shifted back to the main body of people at the table, and I sat wondering. Somehow intuitively I felt a sense that something significant was about to happen. I can't properly explain it except to say that the air felt thicker, and my heart was beating faster.

Several minutes passed, and again he looked over my way with a second, yet redundant question, "Are you sure you aren't a writer?"

In seconds my mind became somewhat sarcastic, thinking, *I think I would know if I was a writer. Writers write things!* But with restraint, I responded, "No...I'm sure."

I felt uncomfortable. Was I responding in the proper way? I had always wanted to be a writer, yet had received no training in it. I had sent a 1,000-word article to a friend of mine who wrote for a magazine, and it came back bleeding with red ink. I had ripped it up and thrown it away determining that this was not a natural gift and that I should pursue other interests. So then I thought, *Maybe I should explain to this peculiar individual that I had tried writing but it didn't seem to pan out.*

Before I could structure my comment to bring clarification, he was visually engaging me again. He said in a cryptic fashion, "Do you know why I'm asking you this?" Inside, my mind was racing as I was trying to determine if this was a trick question. After a quick and obvious response he said, "There's a writer's quill over your head, and everyone that I've seen with that has been a writer."

Oh...that clears everything up! I thought. *A writer's quill is over my head? Is this the way that Heaven speaks?*

The conversation did not come back to me again. I was ruined. Something overwhelmed me at the release of that comment and virtually undid me. Somehow, my destiny was tied up into that comment, and a seed had been planted deep in my spirit that took years to unfold.

The truth is…someone moved my finish line. I now had a greater clarity in my life, yet I didn't know what to do with it. I knew it was from Heaven because of the randomness of the circumstances and the profound impact that it had had on my psyche. That word has aggravated me ever since!

After that, I wrote and published several articles for a couple of magazines, eventually landing a regular column for a year or so. Inside though, I knew that this was not the fulfillment of that word. I grew more frustrated, forsaking and rationalizing this word many times.

Destiny Shaping

I felt haunted by the words of 1990. It was as if they were calling me night and day to a place of fulfillment. It was like a virus that had been downloaded from Heaven and was infecting every decision and position that I took in life.

The word itself began to shape how I thought and communicated. I understood how Joseph felt as misunderstanding after misunderstanding began to mount up to an absolute surrender. I couldn't make this word be fulfilled on my own. It was deposited with a power that worked in all areas of my life. It was like a giant earth mover that was rearranging the landscape of how I thought!

Years passed and more words came regarding writing. It came to a point where regularly someone would say, "I have this sense about you."

He that can have patience can have what he will.

—*Benjamin Franklin*

I wanted to interrupt them and say, "I know, I know, I'm a writer!" I began to understand that it was all in reference to books...the writing of books. I'd never written a book.

WRITE THE BOOK

In 2004, I finally began to write a book. I wrote two chapters and quickly hit a wall. I abandoned the project for several years until January of 2007. I woke up one morning and heard a strong impression say, "Write the book." *Ahhhh!*

Almost 20 years of frustration and challenge were coming to a head. As a response, I went to a local bookstore. Thousands of books lined the shelf on any subject that you might care to know about. It was not encouraging! I asked myself, *Why do we need another book? Thousands of new books are being published every day!* I left discouraged and headed for my office. When I sat down at my computer, I could hardly believe my eyes. My first E-mail was from a publisher asking if I was thinking of writing a book! *Ahh, here it is,* I thought. *Maybe I can have some peace now.*

SLOW BLOSSOMS

Certain words that are spoken from Heaven are to bring a response of action. That would make sense. Other words—like the 1990 word for me—are meant to be encouragements during the difficult road of fulfillment. These are life words, and all you can do is watch them unfold and try to stay out of the way.

This type of word will literally shape you. It may even break you. It is meant to remove something from the inside of you to make way for something new that Heaven wants to insert in you. This may be what John the Baptist spoke about when referring to Heaven's voice in this passage.

...but the friend of the bridegroom, who stands and hears him, rejoices greatly because of the bridegroom's voice. Therefore this joy of mine is fulfilled. He must increase, but I must decrease (John 3:29-30).

This is how it is summed up. Major life words will demand a *decrease* in your life. This speaks of *less of you and more of Heaven.* It appears that you will not even have to be concerned about how it will happen. It will happen. You can make it easy...or you can make it difficult.

When Heaven speaks a word, it demands space to grow. An understanding of how God functions in this type of word will give you the patience you will need as it slowly unfolds.

How Long Will I Wait?

Discouragement seems to come when words of this nature take years to fulfill. We are an instant society. In a short period of time, we have seen computers and Internet access get faster and faster—from dial-up, to DSL, to wireless cable and beyond. I'm always amazed at how frustrated I get when Internet access takes more than a second or two!

Twenty years ago, little of this would have been accessible at all. Suffice it to say, we are a demanding people. The trouble is that we are dealing with an omnipresent God. He has all the time in the world. He has great worldwide access, yet chooses to move slowly at times in order to produce lasting fruit.

Delayed Destinies?

The Bible is filled with examples of people who experienced exactly what you are living: the delayed destiny! Abraham is the father of our faith, and even he had to grow in his understanding of the unfolding word of Heaven. God had promised Abraham that he would have an heir and that his descendants would be as the stars of the sky. Yet the unfolding of that word created some tensions.

Abraham's wife, Sarah, evaluated the circumstances and suggested a path to speed up the process. She suggested that Abraham take on another woman and have a son by her. So, through this other woman, Abraham fathered a son named Ishmael, yet this was not the son who had been promised. The phrase, "birthing an Ishmael," has become synonymous with getting ahead of the purposes of Heaven and trying to "fast track" what has been spoken.

We've all heard the story of the chick that was helped out of its shell. Apparently, helping a chick by cracking its shell actually inhibits its ability to develop properly later on. The muscles that a chick develops through breaking out are also necessary later in the chick's development. Trying to make hatching go faster may jeopardize the very existence of the little bird.

The same is true in humans. Often, we must go through the hard labor of freeing ourselves from confinement and then blossoming in order to develop the "muscles" we will need for leadership in the future. This is why so many people who have had difficult upbringings can serve as seasoned leaders in the future. In this case, the old saying is true: "no pain, no gain."

ANOTHER SHOT AT IT

Abraham apparently learned from his lesson. Later on in life, God required Abraham to sacrifice his promised son Isaac on an altar. Abraham seemed to move at Heaven's bidding without hesitation. A confidence was now on him that God could raise his son from the dead if necessary.

Abraham understood that nothing would stand in the way of the fulfillment of his destiny in his son. God, of course, prevented Abraham from doing this drastic measure of murdering his son and reserved it for expression in *His* only Son, Jesus, centuries later.

Late or on Time?

In referring to Jesus, John says "Word became flesh" (see John 1:14). Jesus' life is a personification of a word from Heaven. Jesus did not appear to be in a hurry. After all, He lived in relative obscurity for 30 years.

In the natural realm, sometimes it appeared that He showed up late. A man named Jairus came to Jesus because his daughter was dying. Jesus turned and began to travel to the location to help, yet was accosted by many along the way. In particular, a woman with a serious condition pushed through the crowd and touched Jesus. She was healed, yet it provided a momentary distraction that proved deadly for the little girl that Jesus was intending to minister to. The report comes to Jesus that He is too late, and she has already died.

Of course, this brings up many questions. Jesus understands this and immediately turns to Jairus and says, *"Do not be afraid; only believe"* (Mark 5:36). Upon arriving at the home, Jesus took the 12-year-old girl by the hand and raised her up.

A Dying Friend

A similar situation occurs when Jesus hears that His good friend Lazarus is dying. When Jesus heard that Lazarus was sick, He stayed two days longer where He was. Lazarus died and emotions were flaring among Lazarus's family and friends. His sisters wondered why Jesus had been delayed. Martha said, *"Lord, if You had been here, my brother would not have died"* (John 11:21). This is a reasonable grief. I've asked this same question many times. In the greater sense, we ask, "Why do bad things happen to good people?" In the lesser sense we ask, "Why have You not fulfilled what You have promised?"

Jesus responds with an answer that settles all questions. He states that He is the "resurrection and the life." This takes Him out of time and reason and into the realm of the impossible. All things are possible with Him...even foiled and soiled destinies! He is not limited by circumstances. He is not limited by how we have messed things up. You can reap as long as you do not faint! (See Galatians 6:9.)

TIME...NO BIG DEAL

Time is not an issue with Heaven. Somehow in the thinking of Heaven, time can be bent, reversed, or fast-forwarded depending on the situation. Many believe that they have missed their destiny and no doubt have made choices that sabotage the earthly possibility. God will only use our ashes as a means to bring His beauty. He cannot be delayed from Heaven's perspective...only ours.

He has made everything beautiful in its time (Ecclesiastes 3:11a).

The Bible refers repeatedly to the "*fullness of the time*" and "*due time*" (Gal. 4:4; Rom. 5:6). Regardless of how it may look, God is always on time. Let's peek briefly into possible ways that God thinks with regard to the development of the spoken word in us. This is one of the paths and processes that God uses.

And not only that, but we also glory in tribulations, knowing that tribulation produces perseverance; and perseverance, character; and character, hope (Romans 5:3-4).

It's a simple path to understand, yet difficult to live. God's reasoning is: Difficulty produces perseverance, which develops character and brings hope. This path is a template that can easily be placed over most biblical characters. They encounter challenge that toughens them with patience and character, which ultimately brings hope.

Patience and perseverance have a magical effect before which difficulties disappear and obstacles vanish.

—John Quincy Adams (1767-1848)

Challenge appears to be necessary for the development of the big words from Heaven in your life. Heaven will speak some things as road signs to your potential. The difficulties will shape you into the vessel you need to become in order to hold that level of Heaven in you.

WHAT HEAVEN DOESN'T TELL YOU

Maybe there are some things that Heaven doesn't tell you...for your own good. The greater the destiny, the greater the development within or beneath. It's like skyscrapers; they need to have deep and well-developed foundations in order to reach the heights that they are designed for.

Is it possible that when Heaven speaks "greater wisdom" to you that it is a hint of what might have to come to create that level of wisdom? What brings greater wisdom? It can come supernaturally from Heaven, or it can come in the form of learning from mistakes…others' and yours!

If Heaven's voice states that you will be touched with unusual love, what might you expect? The unlovely! Learning how to deal with the unlovely is one of the greatest ways to develop a heart of compassion! God loves for us to be trained. It's part of the maturation process that any father celebrates. We love to watch our kids grow up and make right choices. God does too!

Think about this in your own life. Heaven speaks a destiny over you, and the next day all hell breaks loose! When that happens, consider that it might just be the first course in your pursuit of the Master's degree.

Israel was given the assurance of a "Promised Land." They could have easily traveled northeast from Egypt and arrived there quite speedily. God had a different plan. He felt that they weren't quite ready for what He had promised and needed some toughening up. Therefore His way was through the wilderness. This was the shaping of the vessel for the filling of the promise.

Then it came to pass, when Pharaoh had let the people go, that God did not lead them by way of the land of the Philistines, although that was near; for God said, "Lest perhaps the people change their minds when they see war, and return to Egypt." So God led the people around by way of the wilderness of the Red Sea. And the children of Israel went up in orderly ranks out of the land of Egypt (Exodus 13:17-18).

God had concern that war or difficulty might cause Israel to abandon their destiny. He chose the longer route. It was slower yet surer. He may do the same with you…slower yet surer!

EXPLORING THE VOICE QUESTIONS:

1. What are some long-term words from Heaven that you are still waiting to see fulfilled?

2. How has the process of waiting shaped who you are?

3. How does Heaven's timing differ from yours? In your life?

DO IT YOURSELF!

Get in a small group and write all of your names on an index card. Turn the card over and shuffle them. Write down on the cards some impressions, words, or verses that you believe Heaven is speaking over you. Eventually return the cards to see what God may have spoken over other group members.

Chapter Nine

TRUSTING THE VOICE:

Believing in Heaven's Promises

This charge I commit to you, son Timothy, according to the prophecies previously made concerning you, that by them you may wage the good warfare (1 Timothy 1:18).

YEARS ago, I was involved in the starting of a church. Two of my children were very young then...about six and ten. When you start a church, you end up doing everything. Due to the fact that you usually start without a permanent facility, you become responsible for setup, take down, teaching, and oversight. On Sundays, I would leave early to go to the site and set up. My son and daughter, Joshua and Ashley, would go with me to help.

On this particular morning, the two children were already thinking about lunch, which was still hours away. We had recently moved back to the U.S. from Canada, and they had fallen in love with a national fast food chain known as "Taco Bell." They asked me, "Dad, can we go to Taco Bell after church?" It was eight in the morning, and they were already fixated on lunch! I could see that more peace would be maintained if I quickly agreed, so I did.

Hours later the church service was over, and people were filing out of the facility. I had long forgotten about Taco Bell in the busyness of the morning. My children had not forgotten though. They came up to me beaming from ear to ear, and excitement was in the air as they asked, "Are you ready to go to Taco Bell?"

I was now quite tired and tried to persuade them toward a different choice. I said, "Why don't we go home, and I'll build a fire? And we'll have a good meal that Mom prepares." I could tell by the look in their faces that I'd have to come up with something better. I tried to use every form of persuasion that I could come up with, letting them know that I was tired and reminding them what a good cook Mom was! I began to insist that we were going to go home.

They were not satisfied. They began to look at each other and then back at me and say, "But you said Taco Bell!" I tried to reason with them further, yet they grew more determined and began to chant, "Taco Bell! Taco Bell!" People began to look over, as my children kept insisting that I hold to my promise.

Finally, under the pressure of the moment, I gave in: "OK, we'll go to Taco Bell!" They began to scream frantically and dance around.

I was steamed on the way to Taco Bell. I was tired, and I hadn't gotten my way. In that moment, I felt an inaudible voice say to me, "Why don't you ever do that to Me?" It was real enough that its power still hits me today. God was asking me why I don't remind Him of what He has promised. A myriad of memories and thoughts began to fill my mind as I recalled all the promises that had been given to me over the years. God had been faithful, yet still many dreams were left unfulfilled.

Flaming enthusiasm, backed up by horse sense and persistence, is the quality that most frequently makes for success.

—*Dale Carnegie*

REMINDING GOD

It's strange what happened over the next few days. I have found that God speaks to us in series of communications through diverse means. It's almost as if He gets stuck on a topic. He relentlessly and lovingly hammers at a theme in our hearts until we "get it." He will keep reminding you of something that He has said or a truth that He doesn't want you to forget. Everywhere you look, something seems to confirm what He is attempting to communicate. I began to be obsessed with the phrase that my kids had said to me, "You said Taco Bell!" It represented a desperation…a *childlike* trust that if you *said it,* then it *will* come to pass.

I remember one afternoon after that encounter, I was driving through our city's park system praying. My heart was heavy with all of the promises that God had spoken, yet had not been fulfilled. I had run out of things to say to God, having prayed everything I knew to pray. All of a sudden, out of sheer desperation, I rolled down my window and yelled, "You said Taco Bell!" A nearby jogger picked up his pace! I'm not typically given to this type of outburst, yet it seemed so appropriate at the moment.

I prayed that prayer for at least a month, and I still resort back to it periodically. It's like a code between me and God. It's a part of our history together, and He knows exactly what I mean. I'm calling Him on what He has promised.

I was speaking shortly after that at a large gathering in Holland, and I actually used this illustration in a message that I delivered. Several thousand were in attendance, and many came up to me to relate how that story had touched them. That night, several people were speaking testimonies to the crowd about what they had received from the conference. One man from India took his stand and began to talk about all of the challenges that he faced in his native country. I could barely understand much of what he said, but at the end of his talk he said, "I'm going back to India and I will say, 'God, You said Taco Bell!'" The crowd went wild. They knew what he was saying. Desperate people take desperate measures. He was at the end of his rope and cried out to a God who had made him a promise. Apparently desperation is understood in every language. I've wondered and laughed many times about what Indian people would have thought at the statement! I suppose it doesn't matter as long as God knows what is coming from the heart.

God has large shoulders. The Bible says in Isaiah 9:6 that the government will be upon His shoulders. He apparently is able to handle our challenges. We can call Him to account on

His word. We are His children, and He said that we could go to *Taco Bell!* God is a loving father who wants to give good things to His children.

> *Every good gift and every perfect gift is from above, and comes down from the Father of lights, with whom there is no variation or shadow of turning* (James 1:17).

It's appropriate to remind God of the things that He has spoken over you. Let this verse encourage you:

> *This charge I commit to you, son Timothy, according to the prophecies previously made concerning you, that by them you may wage the good warfare* (1 Timothy 1:18).

Words from Heaven are meant to be used as weapons (against the adversary) in your life. Opposition to the fulfillment of your destiny can be expected. Nehemiah was a great builder with a desire to restore the walls of Jerusalem. He methodically and strategically planned every phase. In times like this, only the power of what Heaven has communicated to you will keep you going.

Discouragers came by to observe Nehemiah's progress. They told him that a fox could topple his efforts. Later on, they tried to get him to come and reason in the valley of "Ono." Beware of anyone who wants you to come into the valley of "Ono." Nehemiah discerned that they thought to do him harm. He replied to his enemies by saying, "*I am doing a great work so that*

I cannot come down. Why should the work cease while I leave it and go down to you?" (Neh. 6:3).

The voice from Heaven can and will sustain you through these challenges. You just keep your eyes focused and refuse to step back from the sure word that has been delivered to you. Nehemiah had heard a word, and he was willing to believe God that He would bring it to pass.

Let me tell you the secret that has led me to my goal. My strength lies solely in my tenacity.

— Louis Pasteur (1822-1895)

Other people always have reasons why we should fail. Years ago, as I was planting a church in Canada, I went to the local newspaper to place an advertisement. I explained to the man in charge what I was planning to do. He snickered. When I inquired as to why—he laughed. He said, "Oh, I don't think you'll be around a month from now." Interestingly enough, I lasted ten years, while he was released from his long-held position shortly after that!

King David must have felt similar things when he penned in Psalm 13:1, *"How long, O Lord?"* The questioning of God is legitimate. The reminding of God regarding your unfolding history is essential. The words you hold are tools to remind Heaven and weapons to remind evildoers!

The Old Testament figure, Daniel, stood as a light in a dark captivity. He had been captured and set in a foreign land and forced to heed their laws. Yet, he didn't let the culture influence him. He became the influencer.

Daniel must have felt all alone and far from home. His usual rituals and routines of faith had been outlawed, yet he continued to worship, unaffected by the oppression of his surroundings. In a time of desperation, he cried out to God. Look at the following verse and see how he weaved the past promise with the present reality.

In the first year of Darius the son of Ahasuerus, of the lineage of the Medes, who was made king over the realm of the Chaldeans—in the first year of his reign I, Daniel, understood by the books the number of the years specified by the word of the Lord through Jeremiah the prophet, that He would accomplish seventy years in the desolations of Jerusalem. Then I set my face toward the Lord God to make request by prayer and supplications, with fasting, sackcloth, and ashes. And I prayed to the Lord my God, and made confession, and said, "O Lord, great and awesome God, who keeps His covenant and mercy with those who love Him, and with those who keep His commandments" (Daniel 9:1-4).

Daniel was saying "Taco Bell!" to God! He understood former words that had been spoken by the prophet and turned to remind God of them. He reminded God that He keeps His covenant, or promise.

Daniel's appeal to Heaven released action. Gabriel flew to him and assured him that he would get understanding.

Desperate times should drive us to remind God of all that He has promised.

What has Heaven spoken over your life? What fingerprints are visible in your destiny? Is the dream that Heaven has given you beginning to unfold?

Remind Heaven of what it has promised. Appeal to a Father who loves to bless His children. You may be approaching the last chapter of waiting. The promise is nearer than you might think!

Exploring the Voice Questions:

1. How has God been faithful? Discuss some situations when He has come through for you with a great fulfillment.

2. How do we avoid going into the valley of "Ono"? How do we protect ourselves against the discouragers in our lives?

3. What actions should we take to learn to stand firm while waiting?

Do It Yourself!

Remind Heaven of a promise that you've held onto for years.

Speak into someone's destiny. Add Heaven-sent information to the reservoir of understanding that they already have.

Make a timeline of words or events in your life that point to a destiny.

Form partnerships in a group. Call someone on a cell phone who needs encouragement. Hand the phone to a partner who does not know the person and let them share their impressions from God to them. Focus on encouragement toward their destiny.

Chapter Ten

THE MATURING
OF YOUR VOICE:

*Releasing Your Heaven-Trained
Voice to the World*

Bless and do not curse (Romans 12:14b).

THE imprint of Heaven will eventually impact your own voice. You've probably seen what happens when a group of teens hang around together. They begin to look and talk alike. Couples that have lived together begin to think and dream in similar ways. In many aspects, you become like those whom you choose to put in front of your eyes.

Heaven's values and ways will ultimately become your ways, if your heart is soft and receptive. If you have practiced the principles in this book then your voice is beginning to mature. It is saturated and marinated with the nature of Heaven.

There will even be times when you will naturally and effortlessly speak what is right and appropriate, due to your association with Heaven's voice. The voice of Heaven calls us to submit our senses to transformation.

> *For though by this time you ought to be teachers, you need someone to teach you again the first principles of the oracles of God; and you have come to need milk and not solid food. For everyone who partakes only of milk is unskilled in the word of righteousness, for he is a babe. But solid food belongs to those who are of full age, that is, those who by reason of use have their senses exercised to discern both good and evil* (Hebrews 5:12-14).

Notice the phrase, "*by reason of use*"? The exercise of our lives brings about a "sense-a-tivity." We become trained in discernment from our experience of learning to know His ways.

When I was a trainer in business, we used a progression for learning that shows a gradual self-awareness. We all progress from:

Unconsciously Incompetent — This is the place where you are clueless. You are bad, inept, but have no idea that you are! Take public speaking, for example. You probably have no idea of your many poor habits—like saying "Um" after every phrase, or fidgeting when you're nervous—until someone begins to "coach" you. You may not be able to see your great need for help. Yet the humble heart will move forward and desire to learn. Now you begin to mature, start your training, and move on to:

Consciously Incompetent — This is the phase where you *realize* that you aren't as good as you thought you were.

The veil has been lifted, and a season of humility moves in as you begin to aggressively remake your skills. Progress can be made quickly during this phase, if you are teachable. The next phase is one of maturity.

Unconsciously Competent — Finally, you are getting to a place of maturity. This is the fun part. When I trained people in public speaking, I loved to see them soar. The annoying habits of the past dissolve, and students begin to shine. Skill and excellence become second nature.

The world needs a people who have been trained from Heaven. Their eyes see the good in others. Their ears shut out the evil, destructive words. Most important of all, their mouth is a servant of Heaven. It yields to the flavor and nature of Heaven itself, bringing grace into every situation.

These people of the voice will discern good from evil. They will be accustomed to recognizing its presence and quick to lead into a safe place. They will naturally emerge as leaders in a time of darkness because they have become a light.

The Book of James has stern warnings regarding the mouth.

For we all stumble in many things. If anyone does not stumble in word, he is a perfect man, able also to bridle the whole body. Indeed, we put bits in horses' mouths that they may obey us, and we turn their whole body. Look also at ships: although they are so large and are driven by fierce winds, they are turned by a very small rudder wherever the pilot desires. Even so the tongue is a little member and boasts great things (James 3:2-5a).

Regardless of what great revelations we may receive, we must commit to the challenging task of controlling our tongue. Our tongues must be trained and restrained into an instrument of blessing. How sad it is when cursing proceeds from a vessel crafted to bless.

PROPER USE OF THE MOUTH

A powerful expression for a human voice is the art of blessing. "Blessing" is a religious-sounding word that originates in the same word as "eulogy." Unfortunately, in our culture we give eulogies at funerals. When you think about it, doesn't it seem odd to speak strong, encouraging words when someone is already dead?

The word for blessing literally means a "well word." In the Bible, blessing words were typically spoken over children or groups of people. Blessings had a power that was akin to a word from Heaven yet originated in the human heart. A blessing is the inward desire you have for another human being. Your desires for another are meant to provide a framework, like a trellis channeling a growing vine.

The interesting part about a blessing is that even though it originates with the human heart, it ignites something in Heaven similar to a partnership. Using gambling terms, it is as if Heaven hears what you say and responds by raising the word to another level. Heaven likes life-giving words and treats them as if they are prophetic.

FATHER'S BLESSING

In the summer of 1984, my father blessed me. He called my brother Chris and me into the living room. We knelt down in a ceremonial way, and he placed his hands on our heads. He then spoke to his two, adult sons with words of destiny. These words were his desires for us as his sons.

He spoke of the strengths of our family and imparted an ability to walk wisely for success and riches. It had such an impact on me that I in turn blessed each of my children on their 13th birthdays. I made it special and invited family and friends. It went beyond the usual birthday party with a time of calling all together with a unique focus on each child.

I remember specifically when I blessed my second daughter, Lauren. We had a great party, and the time came to speak the living eulogy. I stood behind her as she was sitting in a chair. After a time of communicating all that I loved about her to the group, I began the blessing.

I spoke of her qualities and ways that I could see her using them in the future. She loves children and the elderly. I told the group that Lauren would work well with helping people of all ages, and compassion would be a weapon and tool for her life.

I then spoke about my family history and my wife's family history, calling her to a challenge to live up to the generations that came before her. There were many tears in the house. I had touched on an emotional nerve in everybody. At the end of the blessing I commissioned her to walk and talk as an adult. I called her to fulfill the mandate and continue the blessing of her ancestors.

Several people at the end asked me if I could do that for them! It appears that there is a child in each one of us that longs for the blessing of the father. Many of the challenges in today's culture may be caused by a lack of direction spoken over a child. Many are wandering souls looking for someone to frame a destiny through kind words. You and I were born to be blessers!

We failed, but in the good providence of God apparent failure often proves a blessing.

—Robert E. Lee (1807-1872)

PRIESTLY BLESSINGS

A priestly blessing was spoken in the Old Testament that serves as a template for contemporary blessings that we might speak. The Lord instructed Moses to:

Speak to Aaron and his sons, saying, "This is the way you shall bless the children of Israel. Say to them: 'The Lord bless you and keep you; the Lord make His face shine upon you, and be gracious to you; the Lord lift up His countenance upon you, and give you peace.'" So they shall put My name on the children of Israel, and I will bless them (Numbers 6:23-27).

Can you see the partnership? Humans are to speak "Heaven-type" words, and then God will establish them. Can you imagine if every family in the world began to speak into the potential of their children? Heaven would affirm the words and establish them as if they originated from Him!

Ancient cultures named their children in such a way as to declare their identity prior to its unfolding. A name had a deeper meaning than it does today and carried a strong sense of destiny on it.

ROBBED DESTINIES

In the Old Testament, the blessing was so powerful that some sought to steal it in order to secure a better future. Jacob tricked his father, Isaac, who had problems with his sight. While his brother Esau was hunting, Jacob schemed to steal the blessing. Esau was the rightful recipient. Jacob masterfully prepared a feast to trick his father and put animal skins on his arms to convince his dad that he was his hairier brother. It worked. He received the strong blessing reserved for the older brother.

Genesis 27:27-29 contains the honorable blessing. He was blessed with prosperity, authority, and a protection from those that would oppose him. Those who blessed him would be blessed, and those who cursed him would be cursed. Apparently, these blessings were so strong that they could not be recanted. A lesser blessing was given to the older brother.

A study of numerous blessings in the Bible indicates that human words actually came to pass with similar accuracy as those originating in Heaven. A generational release of good words can pave the roadway of success.

An old man named Simeon had the honor of blessing Jesus himself. Joseph and Mary brought Jesus to the temple, and this is what Simeon spoke over the child, Jesus, and His parents:

> *"Lord, now You are letting Your servant depart in peace, according to Your word; for my eyes have seen Your salvation which You have prepared before the face of all peoples, a light to bring revelation to the Gentiles, and the glory of Your people Israel." And Joseph and His mother marveled at those things which were spoken of Him. Then Simeon blessed them, and said to Mary His mother, "Behold, this Child is destined for the fall and rising of many in Israel, and for a sign which will be spoken against (yes, a sword will pierce through your own soul also), that the thoughts of many hearts may be revealed"* (Luke 2:29-35).

Simeon spoke things that were to come to pass. They sound prophetic, yet originated in his own spirit.

FAULTY VISION

God loves for us to speak as He would. All fathers do! What a joy it is to hear our children imitating the good things that come from our mouths. What an embarrassment when the opposite happens!

After years of hearing His voice, we develop an ability to speak like Heaven would speak. It becomes supernaturally natural! We take on the very nature of our heavenly Father.

God wants us to see with His eyes. The natural tendency for many of us is to see the faults. For example, when we shop for a vase, we look for a crack. When we shop for a car, we scrutinize every square inch and even kick the tires! We hire inspectors to examine houses that we are about to buy. We want a list of the faults. This is human nature. Unfortunately we do the same thing in assessing one another and ourselves.

When you focus on being a blessing, God makes sure that you are always blessed in abundance.

—Joel Osteen (1963-)

PUZZLING VISION

God has a different slant on things. He sees beyond our surface blemishes and looks into the heart. I remember one time, back when I first got married, I invited a single friend to come over and visit. My wife and I had few furnishings. We had bean bags, wood crate end tables, and no art on the walls…except for some puzzles. We used to spend time putting large 1,000-piece puzzles together. We must have bought cheap puzzles because inevitably we ended up finishing with pieces missing. We hung them on the walls of our small apartment anyway. They brought a sense of color and texture even though they were incomplete.

When my friend walked in, he made the typical comments and made his way into our living area. He noticed the puzzles hung on the wall and said, "Hey, there are missing pieces!" Quite frankly, I had forgotten that there were missing pieces. I guess puzzles are like people, and after a while you overlook the common faults.

I encouraged my friend to look at the bigger picture, without focusing on the missing pieces. He kept shaking his head, not understanding how we would hang something up that was incomplete! Once again, the fault was what caught his eye.

THE WAY GOD SEES IT

A biblical character named Gideon illustrates this point exactly. He was being called of God to take an army and fight against 120,000 enemy soldiers. In Judges 6, a mental battle takes place as God tries to get Gideon to see what He sees. God sees the big picture, and Gideon sees all the challenges (i.e., obstacles).

Now the Angel of the Lord came and sat under the terebinth tree which was in Ophrah, which belonged to Joash the Abiezrite, while his son Gideon threshed wheat in the winepress, in order to hide it from the Midianites. And the Angel of the Lord appeared to him, and said to him, "The Lord is with you, you mighty man of valor!" Gideon said to Him, "O my lord, if the Lord is with us, why then has all this happened to us? And where are all His miracles which our fathers told us about, saying, 'Did not the Lord bring us up from Egypt?' But now the Lord has forsaken us and delivered us into the hands of the Midianites." Then the Lord turned to him and said, "Go in this might of yours, and you shall save Israel from the hand of the Midianites. Have I not sent you?" So he said to Him, "O my Lord, how can I save Israel? Indeed my clan is the weakest in Manasseh, and I am the least in my father's house." And the Lord said to him, "Surely I will be with you, and you shall defeat the Midianites as one man" (Judges 6:11-16).

Do you witness the struggle? God sees the valor and might that is hidden in this young man. Gideon can only see the flaws and cracks. Gideon challenges God to prove Himself in several different ways. He even sneaks into the enemy camp and hears a dream that one of the enemy soldiers has. The soldier expresses fear of Gideon, which then encourages Gideon to move toward battle.

Gideon indeed became what God saw in him from the beginning. He was a valiant warrior. God had to work on his framework of thinking to help him see what he could not see naturally. This is the way God thinks. We see the bad…He sees the good!

A blessing is all about speaking in a fashion of what you know that God would say over someone. As you become familiar with Heaven's ways, you will speak its language. You will bless and not curse. You will speak life and not death. Your words may become so intertwined with Heaven's voice that it becomes difficult to know the difference. Your words will excite Heaven and solicit its involvement. You will speak Heaven on earth. Maybe that's the way it was supposed to be!

Components of the Blessing

A book by Gary Smalley, called *The Blessing*, gives helpful guidelines in releasing words that build. Listed here are five components of the blessing.[1]

1. **Meaningful touch** — It sounds simple, but a touch of the hand on a shoulder gives deep reassurance to the one you are blessing.

2. **Spoken message** — Remember the power of words. Good words spoken over a friend or loved one can actually bring life. Don't hold back...speak life!

3. **Attach high value** — Forget the faults. Every parent or any boss can easily speak of the faults of their child or employee. You know them better than anyone else. Tell them of your love, admiration, and the qualities of who they have become.

4. **Picture a special future** — Speak descriptive words over them of a dynamic future of hope. Remember...speak like Heaven would speak. Paint a verbal picture that has color and purpose. Take your time and be thorough. Act as if you are designing the road that they will travel on. You probably are!

5. **Commit to help fulfill blessing** — Assure them that you will do whatever you can to secure their future. You will be an encourager, cheerleader, counselor,

and in the case of your child, you will financially back them toward their dream.

CADILLAC BLESSINGS

My father spoke many blessings over me. They shaped my life. Many times he would lay his hand on my shoulder and declare what was to be regardless of what I felt. I would be ready to go before a large crowd, and he would pull me aside for a minute and give me a pep talk. He always expressed confidence in my ability when I had none. He also backed his blessing up with his personal commitment to my success.

In the summer of 2001, my father began to inject a proposal into our weekly phone conversations.

He said, "Hey, I want to give you my car."

I responded in a way that I thought was right as a son. I would respond each week, "Dad, I don't need your car...it's yours!"

Frustrated, he would hang up. I didn't want to take advantage of him. He had assisted me many times in my life, demonstrating his ability to back up his words over me.

Well, he didn't back down. Each week, we went through the same scenario. Each week I responded in the same way.

Finally, becoming frustrated, he confronted me, "Hey...what's wrong with you? Why won't you let me give you this car?"

I again responded in the same fashion. As I hung up the phone, I heard an inner voice say, *"What is wrong with you?"*

I felt cut to the heart. I called him right back and said, "When do you want me to pick up the car?"

Within days, I flew to Louisiana to get the brand-new Cadillac that was promised. It was an impacting time as he took the vehicle and had it serviced to make sure it was perfect for my trip back home.

On a dank morning, I rose early and packed my new car. I'll never forget my father coming out into the driveway with his robe on. He had been ill and had lost weight. The powerful man I knew growing up had whittled down to a thin, more peaceful individual.

He said, "I want to bless your new car."

He was following an ancient pattern. He had captured its power and knew that words could shape a destiny. He stretched out his hand and began to speak a Cadillac blessing.

It was an interesting blessing that painted a picture of my family traveling together in the vehicle. He spoke of safety and joy together as we shared this precious gift. He also spoke that I would taste Heaven when I drove in this vehicle. We hugged, and I hit the road.

I think I cried intermittently for the first 200 miles of my journey home. I was overwhelmed with the blessing. He was right. Many months after that gift was given to me, I would feel a presence of Heaven while driving it. Many times, I would become overwhelmed as I recalled the father's blessing on that humid Louisiana morning.

Almost Missed It

I never realized that the trip that I would take with my family in that car would be to his funeral. I almost missed the blessing. This was to be his final blessing to me while he was alive. The car was a great gift, but the action of blessing has stuck with me to this day.

The world is hungry for encouragement. They are wandering in the dark, seeking direction. Heaven's voice is speaking to a new generation. It's calling us to learn its words and speak with its life-giving force. Many voices are filling the air, but in truth only one counts.

Listen to the *voice* of Heaven…

Do It Yourself!

All I can say is…listen…learn…love…

Endnote

1. Gary Smalley and John Trent, *The Blessing* (Thomas Nelson, 2004).

MINISTRY PAGE

Steve Witt offers standard or customized training for businesses and churches in the following subject areas:

Voices — Learning the Language of Heaven

This can contain up to four different modules of three sessions each, with practical activations in hearing the voice of Heaven.

Choices — Establishing a Life Map

This is an interactive training of eight sessions that assist in setting a spiritual map, including goal setting, uncovering your passions, and charting a course.

Noises — Learning the Rhythm of Life

This is a four-session training course in meditation and contemplation. The goal is to center a life, focus it, make it in tune with Heaven. This course includes practical activations with instruction on living a life with less stress and more peace.

Consultation for Public Speakers and Trainers

Professional assessment of public speaking skills through either onsite evaluation or DVD critique. The goal is to enhance existing skills and challenge you to have greater influence and impact through public communication.

Other training for financial stewardship, marital equipping, as well as scheduled speaking for churches, non-profits, and businesses is also available.

Check www.istevewitt.com for other resources and tips for life. Downloadable messages and blog are available, as well as advice for leading a group using *Voices* as a guide.

NOTES

Additional copies of this book and other
book titles from DESTINY IMAGE are
available at your local bookstore.

Call toll free: 1-800-722-6774.

Send a request for a catalog to:

Destiny Image® **Publishers, Inc.**
P.O. Box 310
Shippensburg, PA 17257-0310

*"Speaking to the Purposes of God for this
Generation and for the Generations to Come."*

**For a complete list of our titles,
visit us at www.destinyimage.com**